Japanese

Guaranteed to get you talking

Contents

≡ Special Features

Before You Go

You can have a fantastic time in Japan's major cities without speaking Japanese, but even just a few phrases will help you make friends, attract smiles and advice from locals, and ensure you have a rich and rewarding travel experience. You could experience the best meal of your trip in a hidden-away izakaya, find a tiny art gallery off the tourist trail or taste delicious locally brewed sake.

PRONUNCIATION TIPS

Japanese pronunciation is not considered difficult for English speakers. Unlike some other Asian languages, it has no tones and most of its sounds are also found in English.

★ Vowels in Japanese can be either short or long. The long ones should be held twice as long as the short ones and are represented in our pronunciation guides with a horizontal line on top of them.

★ Most consonant sounds are pretty close to their English counterparts. Pronounce the double consonants with a slight pause between them, as this can change the meaning.

MUST-KNOW GRAMMAR

★ Japanese does not have words equivalent to the English indefinite and definite articles 'a/an' and 'the':

It's a/the hotel. ホテルです。
(lit: hotel is) ho·te·ru des

present positive	です des
present negative	じゃありません ja a·ri·ma·sen
past positive	でした desh·ta
past negative	じゃありません でした ja a·ri·ma·sen desh·ta

4

★ Japanese has various levels of formality. The standard polite ending -mas ます (given in this book) is the safe middle ground, and suitable for most situations

★ As in English, adjectives come before the noun eg: あれはきれいな建物です。 (lit: that-over-there wa beautiful building is) a·re wa ki·rē na ta·te·mo·no des

★ **There is/There are**
There are two ways of expressing that something exists in Japanese. For animate objects (people and animals) the verb i·mas (います) is used. For inanimate objects (things) a·ri·mas (あります) is used.

★ **Possessives** The easiest way to indicate possession is to use the possessive particle no (の) after the noun, pronoun or proper noun that indicates who or what possesses something, eg: **my friend** (私の友達) wa·ta·shi no to·mo·da·chi

SOUNDS FAMILIAR?

Numerous Japanese words are already part of English vocabulary – most of us are familiar with *karaoke, sushi, ramen, anime, sake...*

Fast Talk Japanese

Don't worry if you've never learnt Japanese (日本語 ni·hon·go) before – it's all about confidence. You don't need to memorise endless grammatical details or long lists of vocabulary – you just need to start speaking. You have nothing to lose and everything to gain when the locals hear you making an effort. And remember that body language and a sense of humour have a role to play in every culture.

"you just need to start speaking"

Even if you use the very basics, such as greetings and civilities, your travel experience will be the better for it. Once you start, you'll be amazed how many prompts you'll get to help you build on those first words. You'll hear people speaking, pick up sounds and expressions from the locals, catch a word or two that you know from TV already, see something on a billboard – all these things help to build your understanding.

5 *Phrases* **to Learn Before You Go**

BEFORE YOU GO

1. How do I get to...?
…へはどう行けばいいですか?

. . . e wa dō i·ke·ba ī des ka

Finding a place can be difficult in Japan. Addresses usually give an area, not a street; practice asking directions.

2. What's the local speciality?
地元料理は何がありますか?

ji·mo·to·ryō·ri wa na·ni ga a·ri·mas ka

Throughout Japan most areas have a speciality dish and locals usually love to talk about food.

3. Please bring a (knife/fork/spoon).
(ナイフ/ フォーク/スプーン)をください。

(nai·fu/fō·ku/spūn) o ku·da·sai

If you haven't quite mastered the art of eating with chopstick don't be afraid to ask for cutlery in a restaurant.

4. I'd like a nonsmoking seat, please.
禁煙席をお願いします。

ki·nen·se·ki o o·ne·gai·shi·mas

There are smoking seats in many restaurants and on some bullet trains so be sure to specify if you want smoke-free.

5. Can you recommend any local tourist attractions
地元の観光スポットをお勧めしますか?

ji·mo·to no kan·kō su·pot·to o o su·su·me shi·mas ka

Locals will be happy to recommend places for you to visit, an often will go out of their way to tell you the best way to get there and enjoy it to the fullest.

6

10 Phrases to Sound Like a Local

Great!	すごい!	su·goy
Sure	もちろん	mo·chi·ron
Hey!	ちょっと	cho·to
Just a minute	ちょっと待って	cho·to mat·te
It's OK	いいよ	ī·yo
No problem	大丈夫	dai·jō·bu
Good luck!	頑張って!	gam·bat·te
Seriously?	マジ?	ma·ji
Really?	ほんと?	hon·to
No way!	ありえない!	a·ri·e·nai

10 Phrases to Start a Sentence

What time is (the next bus)?	(次のバスは)何時ですか？ (tsu·gi no bas wa) nan·ji des ka
Where is (the station)?	(駅)はどこですか？ (e·ki) wa do·ko des ka
Where can I (buy a ticket)?	(切符は)どこで(買え)ますか？ (kip·pu wa) do·ko de ka·e·mas ka
Do you have (a map)?	(地図)がありますか？ (chi·zu) ga a·ri·mas ka
Is there (a toilet)?	(トイレ)がありますか？ (toy·re) ga a·ri·mas ka
I'd like (the menu).	(メニュー)をお願いします。 (me·nyū) o o·ne·gai shi·mas
How much is (this dress)?	(このドレス)はいくらですか？ (ko·no do·re·su) wa i·ku·ra des ka
Can I (take a photo)?	(写真を撮って)もいいですか？ (sha·shin o tot·te) mo ī des ka
Do I need a (reservation)?	(予約)が必要ですか？ (yo·ya·ku) ga hi·tsu·yō des ka
Can you (write down the price)?	(値段を書いて)もらえますか？ (ne·dan) o kai·te mo·ra·e·mas·ka

8

Chatting & Basics

⟰ Fast Phrases

Hello/Goodbye	こんにちは/さようなら kon·ni·chi·wa/sa·yō·na·ra
Please/Thank you	ください/ありがとう ku·da·sai/a·ri·ga·tō
Do you speak English?	英語が話せますか？ ē·go ga ha·na·se·mas ka

Essentials

Hello/Hi	こんにちは kon·ni·chi·wa
Goodbye	さようなら sa·yō·na·ra
Yes/No	はい/いいえ hai/ ī·ye
Please (asking)	ください ku·da·sai
Please (offering)	どうぞ dō·zo
Thank you (very much).	(どうも)ありがとう(ございます)。 (dō·mo) a·ri·ga·tō (go·zai·mas)
You're welcome.	どういたしまして dō i·ta·shi·mash·te

Do you speak English?	英語が話せますか? ē·go ga ha·na·se·mas ka
Excuse me (to get attention)	すみません su·mi·ma·sen
Sorry	ごめんなさい go·men·na·sai

Meeting & Greeting

Hello/Hi	こんにちは kon·ni·chi·wa
Good morning	おはよう(ございます) o·ha·yō (go·zai·mas)
Good afternoon	こんにちは kon·ni·chi·wa
Good evening	こんばんは kom·ban·wa
Goodbye/See ya	さようなら / じゃ、また sa·yō·na·ra / ja ma·ta
How are you?	お元気ですか? o·gen·ki des ka
Fine, thanks. And you?	はい、元気です。 あなたは? hai, gen·ki des a·na·ta wa

Titles

Mr/ Ms/Mrs/Miss	…さん san
Sir/Madam	…さま sa·ma

Language Difficulties

Do you speak English?	英語が話せますか？ ē·go ga ha·na·se·mas ka
Does anyone speak English?	どなたが英語が話せますか？ do·na·ta ga ē·go ga ha·na·se·mas·ka
Do you understand?	わかりましたか？ wa·ka·ri·mash·ta·ka
I don't understand.	わかりません。 wa·ka·ri·ma·sen
I speak a little.	少し話せます。 su·ko·shi ha·na·se·mas
What does ... mean?	... はどういう意味ですか？ ... wa dō yū i·mi des ka
Could you please repeat that?	繰り返してくれませんか？ ku·ri·ka·e·shi·te ku·re·ma·sen ka
How do you pronounce this?	これはどう発音しますか？ ko·re wa dō ha·tsu·on shi·mas ka
How do you write ...?	... はどう書きますか？ ... wa dō ka·ki·mas ka
Could you please speak more slowly?	もっとゆっくり話してくれませんか？ mot·to yuk·ku·ri ha·na·shi·te ku·re·ma·sen ka
Slowly, please!	ゆっくり話して。 yuk·ku·ri ha·na·shi·te
Could you please write it down?	書いてくれませんか？ kai·te ku·re·ma·sen ka

Fast Talk

Starting Out

When starting to speak another language, your biggest hurdle is saying aloud what may seem to be just a bunch of sounds. The best way to do this is to memorise a few key words, like 'hello', 'thank you' and 'how much?', plus at least one phrase that's not essential, eg 'how are you', 'see you later' or 'it's very cold/hot' (people love to talk about the weather!). This will enable you to make contact with the locals, and when you get a reply and a smile, it'll also boost your confidence.

Introductions

(Excuse me but) What's your name?	(失礼ですが、)お名前は何ですか?	(shi·tsu·rē des ga) o·na·ma·e wa nan des ka
My name is ...	私の名前は … です。	wa·ta·shi no na·ma·e wa ... des

PHRASE BUILDER

This is my ...	こちらは 私の…です。	ko·chi·ra wa wa·ta·shi no ... des
child	子供	ko·do·mo
colleague	同僚	dō·ryō
friend	友達	to·mo·da·chi
husband/wife	主人／妻	shu·jin/tsu·ma
partner (initmate)	パートナー	pā·to·nā

I'd like to introduce you to ...	…を紹介します。	... o shō·kai shi·mas
I'm pleased to meet you	お会いできてうれしいです。	o·ai de·ki·te u·re·shī des

Personal Details

Where are you from?	どちらから来ましたか?	do·chi·ra ka·ra ki·mash·ta ka

PHRASE BUILDER

I'm from...	… から来ました。	... ka·ra ki·mash·ta
Australia	ストラリア	ō·sto·ra·rya
Canada	カナダ	ka·na·da
New Zealand	ニュージーランド	nyū jī·ran·do
The UK	英国	i·gi·ri·su
The USA	アメリカ	a·me·ri·ka

I'm single	私は独身です。	wa·ta·shi wa do·ku·shin des
I'm married	私は結婚しています。	wa·ta·shi wa kek·kon shi·te i·mas
divorced/ separated	私は離婚しました。	wa·ta·shi wa ri·kon shi·mash·ta

PHRASE BUILDER

Here's my ...	これが私の…	ko·re ga wa·ta·shi no...
What's your ...	あなたの…は 何ですか?	a·na·ta no ... wa nan des ka
phone number	電話番号	den·wa·ban·gō
email address	メールアド レス	mē·ru·a·do·res
address	住所	jū·sho

CHATTING & BASICS

13

Occupations & Study

PHRASE BUILDER

I'm a/an...	私は …です。	wa·ta·shi wa ... des
office worker	会社員	kai·sha·in
student/university student	学生/大学生	ga·ku·sei/dai·ga·ku·sei
retired	退職者です	ji·ē·gyō·sha des
self-employed	自営業者	shi·tsu·gyō·sha des

What are you studying?	何を勉強していますか？ na·ni o ben·kyō shi·te i·mas ka

PHRASE BUILDER

I'm studying...	…を勉強 しています	... o ben·kyō shi·tei·mas
science	自然科学	shi·zen·ka·ga·ku
humanities	人文科学	jin·bun·ka·ga·ku
business	ビジネス	bi·ji·nes

Age

How old are you?	おいくつですか？ o·i·ku·tsu des ka
How old is your (daughter/son)?	(息子/娘)さんは おいくつですか？ (mu·su·ko/mu·su·me)·san wa o·i·ku·tsu des ka

14

| I'm ... years old | 私は…歳です。
wa·ta·shi wa ...sai des |
| He/she is ... years old | 彼/彼女は…歳です。
ka·re/ ka·no·jo wa ...sai des |

Interests

| What do you do in your spare time? | ひまなとき何をしますか？
hi·ma na to·ki na·ni o shi·mas ka |

PHRASE BUILDER

I like...	…が好きです。	...ga su·ki des
cooking	料理	ryo·ri
dancing	踊り	o·do·ri
music	音楽	on·ga·ku
movies	映画	ē·ga
shopping	買い物	kai·mo·no

| Do you like ...? | …が好きですか？
... ga su·ki des ka |
| I don't like (...) very much | …があんまり好きじゃない。
...ga an·ma·ri su·ki ja nai |

PHRASE BUILDER

Do you...	…ますか？	...mas ka
go to concerts	ライブに行き	rai·bu ni i·ki
listen to music	音楽を聴き	on·ga·ku o ki·ki
play an instrument	楽器を演奏し	gak·ki o en·sō shi

What bands do you like?	どんなバンドが好きですか？
	don·na ban·do ga su·ki des ka
What music do you like?	どんな音楽が好きですか？
	don·na on·ga·ku ga su·ki des ka
Do you like movies?	映画がすきですか？
	ei·ga ga su·ki
What kind of movies do you like?	どんな映画が好きですか？
	don·na ei·ga ga su·ki des ka

Feelings

PHRASE BUILDER

I'm ...	私は…です。	wa·ta·shi wa ... des
cold	寒い	sa·mui
hot	暑い	at·sui
happy	嬉しい	u·re·shī
thirsty	喉が渇いた	no·do ga ka·wa·i·ta
sad	悲しいです	ka·na·shī
well	元気	gen·ki

I'm hungry	お腹が空いています。
	o·na·ka ga sui·te·i·mas
I'm tired	私は 疲れました。
	wa·ta·shi wa tsu·ka·re·mash·ta
I'm in a hurry	私は急いでね。
	wa·ta·shi wa i·soi·de·ne

Numbers

Cardinal Numbers

The numbers 4, 7 and 9 – and all other numbers containing these numbers – have alternative pronunciations that are completely interchangeable.

1	一	i·chi
2	二	ni
3	三	san
4	四	shi/yon
5	五	go
6	六	ro·ku
7	七	shi·chi/na·na
8	八	ha·chi
9	九	ku/kyū
10	十	jū
11	十一	jū·i·chi
12	十二	jū·ni
20	二十	ni·jū
21	二十一	ni·jū·i·chi
22	二十二	ni·jū·ni
30	三十	san·jū
40	四十	yon·jū
50	五十	go·jū
60	六十	ro·ku·jū
70	七十	na·na·jū
80	八十	ha·chi·jū
90	九十	kyū·jū
100	百	hya·ku

CHATTING & BASICS

200	二百	ni·hya·ku
300	三百	sam·bya·ku
1,000	千	sen
10,000	一万	i·chi·man
1,000,000	百万	hya·ku·man
100,000,000	一億	i·chi·o·ku

Ordinal Numbers

1st	一番	i·chi·ban
2nd	二番	ni·ban
3rd	三番	sam·ban

Useful Amounts

How many?	どのくらい?	do·no ku·rai
How much?	いくつ?	i·ku·tsu
a little	ちょっと	chot·to
a lot/many	たくさん	ta·ku·san
(100) grams	(100)グラム	hya·ku·gu·ra·mu
a kilo	1キロ	i·chi·ki·ro
a half	半分	ham·bun
all	全部	zem·bu
none	なし	na·shi

Time

| What time is it? | 何時ですか?
nan·ji des ka |
| It's (ten) o'clock. | (10)時です。
(jū)·ji des |

Five past (ten).	(10)時5分です。	(jū)·ji go·fun des
Quarter past (ten).	(10)時15分です。	(jū)·ji jū·go·fun des
Half past (ten).	(10)時半です。	(jū)·ji han des
Quarter to (ten).	(10)時15分前です。	(jū)·ji jū·go·fun ma·e des
Twenty to (ten).	(10)時20分前です。	(jū)·ji ni·jup·pun ma·e des
At what time ...?	何時に…？	nan·ji ni ...
At (ten).	(10時)に。	(jū·ji) ni

am	午前	go·zen
pm	午後	go·go
morning	朝	a·sa
day	日中	nit·chū
midday	正午	shō·go
afternoon	午後	go·go
evening	夕方	yū·ga·ta
midnight	真夜中	ma·yo·na·ka
night	夜	yo·ru

Days

Monday	月曜日	ge·tsu·yō·bi
Tuesday	火曜日	ka·yō·bi
Wednesday	水曜日	su·i·yō·bi
Thursday	木曜日	mo·ku·yō·bi

Friday	金曜日	kin·yō·bi
Saturday	土曜日	do·yō·bi
Sunday	日曜日	ni·chi·yō·bi

Months

January	1月	i·chi·ga·tsu
February	2月	ni·ga·tsu
March	3月	san·ga·tsu
April	4月	shi·ga·tsu
May	5月	go·ga·tsu
June	6月	ro·ku·ga·tsu
July	7月	shi·chi·ga·tsu
August	8月	ha·chi·ga·tsu
September	9月	ku·ga·tsu
October	10月	jū·ga·tsu
November	11月	jū·i·chi·ga·tsu
December	12月	jū·ni·ga·tsu
summer	夏	na·tsu
autumn	秋	a·ki
winter	冬	fu·yu
spring	春	ha·ru

Tenses

Present

| now | 今 | i·ma |
| this afternoon | 今日の午後 | kyō no go·go |

this morning	今朝	ke·sa
this month	今月	kon·ge·tsu
this week	今週	kon·shū
this year	今年	ko·to·shi
today	今日	kyō
tonight	今夜	kon·ya

Past

(three days) ago	(3日)前	(mik·ka) ma·e
day before yes-terday	おととい	o·to·toy
last month	先月	sen·ge·tsu
last night	ゆうべ	yū·be
last week	先週	sen·shū
last year	去年	kyo·nen
since (May)	(5月)から	(go·ga·tsu) ka·ra
yesterday	きのう	ki·nō

Future

day after tomorrow	あさって	a·sat·te
in (six days)	(6日)後	(mu·i·ka) go
next ...	来…	rai ...
next month	来月	rai·ge·tsu
next week	来週	rai·shū
next year	来年	rai·nen
tomorrow	明日	a·shi·ta
until (June)	(6月)まで	(ro·ku ga·tsu) ma·de

Weather

What's the weather like?	天気はどうですか？	ten·ki wa dō·des ka?
What's the weather forecast?	天気予報はどうですか？	ten·ke·yo·hō wa dō·des ka?
Today is ...	今日は … です。	kyō wa ... des

PHRASE BUILDER

Will it be ... tomorrow?	明日は … でしょうか？	ash·ta wa ... de·shō ka
cold	寒い	sa·mui
raining	雨が降る	a·me·ga·fu·ru
snowing	雪が降る	yu·ki·ga·fu·ru
sunny	晴れ	ha·re
warm	暖かい	a·ta·ta·kai
windy	風がなる	ka·ze ga na·ru

Directions

Where's ...?	… はどこですか？	... wa do·ko des ka
What's the address?	住所は何ですか？	jū·sho wa nan des ka
How do I get there?	そこへはどう行けばいいですか？	so·ko e wa dō i·ke·ba ī des ka
Can you show me (on the map)?	(地図で)教えてくれませんか？	(chi·zu de) o·shi·e·te ku·re·ma·sen ka
What (street) is this?	この(道路)の名前は何ですか？	ko·no (dō·ro) no na·ma·e wa nan des ka

Fast Talk

Character Styles

Written Japanese is actually a combination of three different scripts. The first, kanji, consists of ideographic characters. The other two, hiragana and katakana, are syllabic scripts – each character represents a syllable.

Kanji are ideographs (symbols that each represent a concept, idea or thing as well as pronunciation, rather than a word or set of words) borrowed from Chinese, eg 本 (hon) for 'book' and 日本語 (ni·hon·go) for 'Japanese language'. Hiragana is used to represent particles and grammatical endings particular to Japanese and are placed alongside the kanji – one single word can contain both scripts.

For example:

| **Where's the market?** | 市場はどこですか? |
| | i·chi·ba wa do·ko des ka |

To see all the characters in the hiragana and katakana alphabets, refer to our kana table on p94.

Colours

red	赤い	a·kai
yellow	黄色い	kī·roy
blue	青い	a·oy
green	緑の	mi·do·ri no
pink	ピンクの	pin·ku no
orange	オレンジ	o·ren·ji
purple	紫の	mu·ra·sa·ki no
silver	銀	gin
gold	金	kin
black	黒い	ku·roy
white	白い	shi·roy

23

Airport & Transport

≡ Fast Phrases

What time is the next bus?	次のバスは何時ですか? tsu·gi no bas wa nan·ji des ka
Does it stop at (Yokohama)?	(横浜)に停まりますか? (yo·ko·ha·ma) ni to·ma·ri·mas ka
A ticket (to Tokyo), please	(東京行き)の切符を ください。 tō·kyō·yu·ki no kip·pu o ku·da·sai

At the Airport

I'm here for ... days.	私は ...日滞在します。 wa·ta·shi wa ... ni·chi tai·zai shi·mas
I'm here for ... weeks.	私は ...週滞在します。 wa·ta·shi wa ...shū tai·zai shi·mas
I'm in transit.	トランジットです。 to·ran·jit·to des
I'm on business/holiday	ビジネス/休暇です。 bi·ji·nes/kyū·ka des
I'm staying at (Hotel Nikko).	(日航ホテル)に泊まります。 (nik·kō·ho·te·ru) ni to·ma·ri·mas

I have nothing to declare.	何も申請するものがありません。 na·ni mo shin·sē su·ru mo·no ga a·ri·ma·sen
I have something to declare	申請するものがあります。 shin·sē su·ru mo·no ga a·ri·mas
That's not mine.	それは私のじゃありません。 so·re wa wa·ta·shi no ja a·ri·ma·sen

Getting Around

PHRASE BUILDER

At what time does the...leave?	何時に...は 出ますか？	nan·ji ni...wa de·mas ka?
boat	ボート	bō·to
bus	バス	ba·su
plane	飛行機	hi·kō·ki
train	電車	den·sha

Which ... goes to (Kyoto)?	(京都)行きの... はどれですか？ (kyō·to)·yu·ki no ... wa do·re des ka
What time does it leave?	何時に出ますか？ nan·ji ni de·mas ka
What time is the next bus?	次のバスは何時ですか？ tsu·gi no bas wa nan·ji des ka
What time is the last bus?	最終のバスは何時ですか？ sai·shū no bas wa nan·ji des ka
Can we get there by public transport?	そこに公共交通機関 で行けますか？ so·ko ni kō·kyō·kō·tsū·ki·kan de i·ke·mas ka

25

Finding your Way

If you're not sure which train to catch, don't be afraid to ask at a ticket desk, and staff will suggest the best routes. Let them know where you want to go:

| I would like to go to (Kyoto), which is the best route? | (京都)に行きたいですが、どちらが最善のルートですか？
Kyō·to ni i·ki·tai·des·ga,
do·chi·ra ga sai·zen no rū·to des ka |

Buying Tickets

| Where do I buy a ticket? | 切符はどこで買えますか？
kip·pu wa do·ko de ka·e·mas ka |

PHRASE BUILDER

A ... ticket please.	…の切符ください。	... no kip·pu ku·da·sai
child's	子ども 料金の	ko·do·mo ryō·kin no
student's	学生料金の	gak·sē ryō·kin no
one-way	片道	ka·ta·mi·chi
return	往復	ō·fu·ku
green-class (train)	グリーン席	gu·rīn·se·ki
ordinary-class (train)	普通席	fu·tsū·se·ki

| Do I need to book? | 予約が必要ですか？
yo·ya·ku ga hi·tsu·yō des ka |
| How long does the trip take? | 時間はどのくらいかかりますか？
ji·kan wa do·no·ku·rai ka·ka·ri·mas ka |

Is it a direct route?	直行便ですか? chok·kō·bin des ka
A ticket (to Tokyo), please.	(東京行きの)切符をください。 (tō·kyō·yu·ki no) kip·pu o ku·da·sai

Luggage

Where can I find a luggage locker?	ロッカーはどこですか? rok·kā wa do·ko des ka
My luggage has been lost.	私の手荷物がなくなりました。 wa·ta·shi no te·ni·mo·tsu ga na·ku·na·ri·mash·ta
My luggage has been damaged.	私の手荷物が壊れました。 wa·ta·shi no te·ni·mo·tsu ga ko·wa·re·mash·ta
My luggage has been stolen.	私の手荷物がぬすまれました。 wa·ta·shi no te·ni·mo·tsu ga nu·su·ma·re·mash·ta

Bus & Train

Please tell me when we get to (Osaka).	(大阪)に着いたら教えてください。 (ō·sa·ka) ni tsu·i·ta·ra o·shi·e·te ku·da·sai
Please stop here.	ここで停めてください。 ko·ko de to·me·te ku·da·sai
That's my seat.	それは私の席です。 so·re wa wa·ta·shi no se·ki des
Is this seat free?	この席は空いていますか。 ko·no se·ki wa ai·te i·mas ka
I'd like to get off at (Kurashiki).	(倉敷)で下車します。 (ku·ra·shi·ki) de ge·sha shi·mas
Does it stop at (Yokohama)?	(横浜)に停まりますか? (yo·ko·ha·ma) ni to·ma·ri·mas ka

What station is this?	ここは何駅ですか? ko·ko wa nan·e·ki des ka
What's the next station?	次は何駅ですか? tsu·gi wa na·ni·e·ki des ka
Do I need to change?	乗り換えなければ いけませんか? no·ri·ka·e·na·ke·re·ba i·ke·ma·sen ka
Can I use this ticket on the (Toei) line?	この切符で(都営)線に 乗れますか? ko·no kip·pu de (to·ē)·sen ni no·re·mas ka
Where's the (east) exit?	(東)口はどこですか? (higa·shi)·gu·chi wa do·ko des·ka

Taxi

Where's the taxi rank?	タクシー乗り場はどこですか? tak·shī·no·ri·ba wa do·ko des ka
I'd like a taxi at (9) o'clock.	(9)時にタクシーをお願いします (ku)·ji ni tak·shī o o·ne·gai shi·mas
How much is it (to ...)?	(…まで)いくらですか? (... ma·de) i·ku·ra des ka
✂ To ...	…まで ... ma·de
Please take me to (this address).	(この住所)までお願い します。 (ko·no jū·sho) ma·de o·ne·gai shi·mas
Please stop here.	ここで停まってください。 ko·ko de to·mat·te ku·da·sai
Please wait here.	ここで待ってください。 ko·ko de mat·te ku·da·sai

Car & Motorbike

Is this the road to (Sapporo)?	この道は(札幌)まで行きますか? ko·no mi·chi wa (sap·po·ro) ma·de i·ki·mas ka
(How long) Can I park here?	(どのくらい)ここに駐車 できますか? (do·no·ku·rai) ko·ko ni chū·sha de·ki·mas ka
Where's a petrol station?	ガソリンスタンドは どこですか? ga·so·rin·stan·do wa do·ko des ka

PHRASE BUILDER

I'd like to hire a ...	…を借りたいの ですが	... o ka·ri·tai no des ga
car	自動車	ji·dō·sha
motorbike	オートバイ	ō·to·bai
How much for daily/weekly hire?	1日/1週間 借りると いくらですか?	i·chi·ni·chi / is·shū·kan ka·ri·ru to i·ku·ra des ka

Cycling

I'd like to hire a bicycle.	自転車を借りたいのですが ji·ten·sha o ka·ri·tai no des ga
Is there a bicycle path?	自転車道がありますか? ji·ten·sha·dō ga a·ri·mas ka
I have a puncture.	パンクしました。 pan·ku shi·mash·ta

Accommodation

≡ Fast Phrases

I have a reservation.	予約があります yo·ya·ku ga a·ri·mas
When is breakfast served?	朝食はいつですか? chō·sho·ku wa i·tsu des ka
What time is checkout?	チェックアウトは何時ですか? chek·ku·ow·to wa nan·ji des ka

Finding Accommodation

Can you recommend a (hotel)?	おすすめの(ホテル)が ありますか? o·su·su·me no ho·te·ru ga a·ri·mas ka
Can you recommend somewhere nearby?	おすすめの近くの ころはありますか? o·su·su·me no chi·ka·ku no to·ko·ro wa a·ri·mas ka

PHRASE BUILDER

Where's a ...?	...がありますか?	... ga a·ri·mas ka
hotel	ホテル	ho·te·ru
japanese-style inn	旅館	ryo·kan
hostel	ホステル	ho·su·te·ru

Finding Somewhere to Stay

Can you recommend somewhere (cheap)?	おすすめの(安い)ところ はありますか? o·su·su·me no (ya·su·i) to·ko·ro wa a·ri·mas ka
Can you recommend somewhere (nearby)?	おすすめの(近くの)ところ はありますか? o·su·su·me no (chi·ka·ku no) to·ko·ro wa a·ri·mas ka
Can you recommend a traditional ryokan?	おすすめの伝統的な 旅館はありますか? o susume no dentō-tekina ryokan wa a·ri·mas ka

Booking & Checking In

I have a reservation.	予約があります yo·ya·ku ga a·ri·mas

	Are there rooms?	空き部屋はありますか? a·ki he·ya wa a·ri·mas·ka

PHRASE BUILDER

Do you have a (...) room?	...ルームはありま すか?	..rū·mu wa a·ri·mas ka
double	ダブル	da·bu·ru
single	シングル	shin·gu·ru
twin	ツイン	tsu·in

How much is it per night?	1泊いくらですか? ip·pa·ku i·ku·ra des ka

ACCOMMODATION

31

For (three) nights/weeks.	(3)泊/週間。 (san)·pa·ku/·shū·kan
From (July 2) to (July 6).	(7月2日)から(7月6日)まで。 (shi·chi·ga·tsu fu·tsu·ka) ka·ra (shi·chi·ga·tsu mu·i·ka) ma·de
Can I see the room?	部屋を見てもいいですか? he·ya o mi·te mo ī des ka
I'll take it.	この部屋にします。 ko·no he·ya ni shi·mas

Requests & Queries

When is breakfast served?	朝食はいつですか? chō·sho·ku wa i·tsu des ka
Please wake me at (seven) o'clock.	(7)時に起こしてください。 (shi·chi)·ji ni o·ko·shi·te ku·da·sai
Could I have (...) please?	… をお願いします。 ... o o·ne·gai shi·mas
Could I have my key, please?	鍵をお願いします。 ka·gi o o·ne·gai shi·mas
Is there Wi-Fi access here?	ここはWi-Fiがありますか? ko·ko de wai·fai ga a·ri·mas ka
Do you have an elevator?	エレベーターがありますか? e·re·bē·tā ga a·ri·mas ka
Do you have a safe?	金庫がありますか? kin·ko ga a·ri·mas ka
Do you arrange tours here?	ここでツアーに申し込めますか? ko·ko de tsu·ā ni mō·shi·ko·me·mas ka
I'm locked out of my room.	部屋に鍵を残したまま 鍵をかけてしまいました。 he·ya ni ka·gi o no·ko·shi·ta ma·ma ka·gi o ka·ke te shi·mai·mash·ta

Fast Talk

Using Patterns

Look out for patterns of words or phrases that stay the same, even when the situation changes, eg 'Do you have ...?' or 'I'd like to ...' (see p8). If you can recognise these patterns, you're already halfway there to creating a full phrase. The dictionary will help you put other words together with these patterns to convey your meaning – even if it's not completely grammatically correct in all contexts, the dictionary form will always be understood.

Complaints

PHRASE BUILDER

It's too...	…すぎます。	su·gi·mas
dark	暗	ku·ra
small	小さ	chī·sa
noisy	うるさ	u·ru·sa

I can't connect to the Wi-Fi in my room.	部屋のWi-Fiに接続できません。 he·ya no wai·fai ni se·tsu·zo·ku de·ki·ma·sen
The (air conditioner) doesn't work.	(エアコン)が壊れています。 e·a·kon ga ko·wa·re·te i·mas
The (fan) doesn't work.	(扇風機)が壊れています。 (sem·pū·ki) ga ko·wa·re·te i·mas
Can I get another (blanket)?	(毛布)をもう一つお願い できますか? (mō·fu) o mō hi·to·tsu o·ne·gai de·ki·mas ka
This (pillow) isn't clean.	この(枕)はきれい じゃありません。 ko·no (ma·ku·ra) wa ki·rē ja a·ri·ma·sen

Saying Thank You

A polite way to say thank you to the hotel staff/your hosts upon checking out is お世話になりました！ (o·se·wa·ni na·ri·mash·ta), which means literally 'I was in your care'!

Checking Out

What time is checkout?	チェックアウトは何時 ですか?
	chek·ku·ow·to wa nan·ji des ka
Can I leave my bags here?	ここで荷物を預かって もらえますか?
	ko·ko de ni·mo·tsu o a·zu·kat·te mo·ra·e·mas ka
Can you call a taxi for me?	タクシーを呼んでもらえますか?
	tak·shī o yon·de mo·ra·e·mas ka
I'll recommend it to my friends.	友達に薦めます。
	to·mo·da·chi ni su·su·me·mas

Eating & Drinking

Fast Phrases

Can I see the menu, please?	ニューをお願いします。	me·nyū o o·ne·gai shi·mas
Can you bring me ..., please?	…をください。	... o ku·da·sai
I'd like the bill, please	お勘定をください。	o·kan·jō o ku·da·sai

Meals

breakfast	朝食/朝ごはん	chō·sho·ku/a·sa·go·han
lunch	昼食/昼ごはん	chū·sho·ku/hi·ru·go·han
dinner	夕食/晩ごはん	yū·sho·ku/ban·go·han
snack	間食/スナック	kan·sho·ku/su·nak·ku
to eat	食べます	ta·be·mas
to drink	飲みます	no·mi·mas

Finding a Place to Eat

Can you recommend a ...?	どこかいい…を 知っていますか?	do·ko ka ī ... o shit·te i·mas ka
cafe	カフェ	ka·fe
restaurant	レストラン	res·to·ran
bar	バー	bā

Local Knowledge

Restaurants

Where would you go for local specialities?	名物を食べるなら どこに 行きますか? mē·bu·tsu o ta·be·ru na·ra do·ko ni i·ki·mas ka
Where would you go for a celebration?	お祝いをするならどこに 行きいますか? oy·wai o su·ru na·ra do·ko ni i·ki·mas ka
Where would you go for a cheap meal?	安い食事をするなら どこに 行きいますか? ya·su·i sho·ku·ji o su·ru na·ra do·ko ni i·ki·mas ka

Are you still serving food?	まだ食事ができますか? ma·da sho·ku·ji ga de·ki·mas ka
For two, please.	2人です。 fu·ta·ri des
How long is the wait?	どのくらい待ちますか? do·no ku·rai ma·chi·mas ka
I'd like to reserve a table for (two people).	(2人)の予約をお 願いします。 fu·ta·ri no yo·ya·ku o o·ne·gai shi·mas
I'd like to reserve a table for (eight) o'clock.	(8)時の予約を お願いします。 (ha·chi)·ji no yo·ya·ku o o·ne·gai shi·mas
I'd like nonsmoking, please.	禁煙席をお願いします。 kin·en·se·ki o o·ne·gai shi·mas

Ordering & Paying

What would you recommend?	なにがお勧めですか？ na·ni ga o·su·su·me des ka
I'd like a local speciality.	地元の名物をお願いします。 ji·mo·to no mē·bu·tsu o o·ne·gai shi·mas
I'll have that (indicating)	あれをください。 a·re o ku·da·sai

PHRASE BUILDER

Please bring ...	...をください	... o ku·da·sai
a knife/fork/ spoon	ナイフ/フォーク/ スプーン	nai·fu/fō·ku/ spūn
a glass	グラス	gu·ra·su
a serviette	ナプキン	na·pu·kin

I'd like the bill, please.	お勘定をください。 o·kan·jō o ku·da·sai
There's a mistake in the bill.	請求書に間違いがあります。 sē·kyū·sho ni ma·chi·gai ga a·ri·mas

Special Diets & Allergies

Is there a halal restaurant?	イスラム教徒のためのハラル レストランはありますか？ i·su·ra·mu·kyō·to no ta·me no ha·ra·ru res·to·ran wa a·ri·mas ka
Is there a kosher restaurant?	ユダヤ教徒のためのコーシャー レストランはありますか？ yu·da·ya·kyō·to no ta·me no kō·shā res·to·ran wa a·ri·mas ka

Fast Talk

Practising

If you want to practise your language skills,
try the waiters at a restaurant. Find your feet with straight-
forward phrases such as asking for a table and ordering
a drink, then initiate a conversation by asking for menu
recommendations or asking how a dish is cooked. And as
you'll often know food terms even before you've 'officially'
learnt a word of the language, you're already halfway to
understanding the response.

Is there a vegetarian restaurant?	ベジタリアンレストランはありますか？	be·ji·ta·ri·an res·to·ran wa a·ri·mas ka
I'm a vegan.	私は厳格な 菜食主義者です。	wa·ta·shi wa gen·ka·ku na sai·sho·ku·shu·gi·sha des
I'm a vegetarian.	私はベジタリアンです。	wa·ta·shi wa be·ji·ta·ri·an des
I'm allergic to ...	私は…にアレルギーがあります。	wa·ta·shi wa ... ni a·re·ru·gī ga a·ri·mas
Could you prepare a meal without ...?	…抜きの料理をお願いできますか？	... nu·ki no ryō·ri o o·ne·gai de·ki·mas·ka

Nonalcoholic Drinks

(cup of) tea	紅茶(1杯)	kō·cha (ip·pai)
(cup of) coffee	コーヒー(1杯)	kō·hī (ip·pai)
with (milk)	(ミルク)入り	(mi·ru·ku)·i·ri
without (sugar)	(砂糖)なし	(sa·tō)·na·shi
orange juice	オレンジジュース	o·ren·ji jū·su
soft drink	ソフトドリンク	so·fu·to do·rin·ku
water	水	mi·zu

Alcoholic drinks

beer	ビール	bī·ru
champagne	シャンペン	sham·pen
cocktail	カクテル	ka·ku·te·ru
a shot of whisky	ウィスキーをワンショット	wis·kī o wan·shot·to
a glass/bottle of ... wine	…ワインをグラス/ボトルで	...wain o gu·ra·su/bo·to·ru de
red	赤	a·ka
rosé	ロゼ	ro·ze
white	白	shi·ro
sparkling	スパークリング	spā·ku·rin·gu

In the Bar

I'll buy you a drink.	1杯おごります。	ip·pai o·go·ri·mas
What would you like?	何を飲みますか?	na·ni o no·mi·mas ka
I'll have ...	…をお願いします。	... o o·ne·gai shi·mas
Same again, please.	同じのをお願いします。	o·na·ji no o o·ne·gai shi·mas
It's my round next.	次は私の番です。	tsu·gi wa wa·ta·shi no ban des
Cheers!	乾杯!	kam·pai

Buying Food

How much is a kilo of ...?	… 1キロいくらですか?	(...) i·chi·ki·ro i·ku·ra des ka
What's the local speciality?	地元料理は何がありますか?	ji·mo·to·ryō·ri wa na·ni ga a·ri·mas ka
What's that?	それは何ですか?	so·re wa nan des ka
How much?	いくら?	i·ku·ra
Can I taste it?	味見してもいいですか?	a·ji·mi shi·te mo ī des ka

PHRASE BUILDER

I'd like ...	…ください	... ku·da·sai
(200) grams	(200)グラム	(ni·hya·ku)·gu·ra·mu
(two) kilos	(2)キロ	(ni)·ki·ro
(three) pieces	(3)個	(san)·ko
(six) slices	(6)枚	(ro·ku)·mai
This/that one	これ/あれを	ko·re/a·re o

Less.	少なく。	su·ku·na·ku
A bit more.	もうちょっと多く。	mō chot·to ō·ku
Enough.	充分です。	jū·bun des

EATING & DRINKING

Menu Decoder
料理読本

The Japanese dishes and ingredients in this menu decoder are listed alphabetically, by pronunciation, so you can easily understand what's on offer in Japanese eateries and ask for what takes your fancy.

~ a ~

a·bo·ga·do アボガド avocado

a·bu·ra 油 oil

…·a·ge …揚げ fried …

a·ge·da·shi·dō·fu 揚げだし豆腐 deep-fried tō·fu in fish stock

a·ge·mo·no 揚げ物 deep-fried food

a·hi·ru アヒル duck

ais·ku·rī·mu アイスクリーム ice cream

a·mai 甘い sweet (taste)

a·ma·za·ke 甘酒 sweet, warm sa·ke

a·me 飴 candy • lolly

am·mi·tsu あんみつ dessert of fruit, diced Japanese jelly & an·ko with syrup on top

am·pan アンパン baked bun filled with an·ko

an あん sweet bean paste

an·ko 餡子 a·zu·ki beans boiled with sugar

a·tsu·a·ge 厚揚げ fried tō·fu

a·wa·bi あわび abalone

a·zu·ki 小豆 red bean – ingredient for the sweet bean paste

~ b ~

ban·cha 番茶 everyday tea

ba·ni·ra バニラ vanilla

ba·ni·ku 馬肉 horse meat

bas バス bass • sea perch

ba·tā バター butter

bē·kon ベーコン bacon

ben·tō 弁当 lunch box normally containing rice with different vegetables, meat, fish & sometimes fruit

be·rī ベリー berries

bī·fu ビーフ beef

bī·fu·ka·tsu ビーフカツ beef cutlet

bi·fu·te·ki ビフテキ beef steak

bī·ru ビール beer • ale

bu·dō ブドウ grapes

bu·ri ブリ amberjack • yellowtail

41

bu·rok·ko·rī ブロッコリー broccoli

bu·ta·ni·ku 豚肉 pork

~ c ~

chā·han チャーハン fried rice

cham·pon チャンポン noodle soup

cha no yu 茶の湯 tea ceremony

chā·shū·men チャーシュー麺 rā·men topped with sliced roast pork

cha·wan·mu·shi 茶碗蒸 savoury steamed egg custard

chip·pu チップ chips (crisps)

chi·ra·shi·zu·shi ちらしずし sushi rice topped with raw fish, a·bu·ra·a·ge & vegetables

chī·zu チーズ cheese

cho·ko·rē·to チョコレート chocolate

chū·hai 酎ハイ shō·chū served with various nonalcoholic mixers

~ d ~

dai·fu·ku·mo·chi 大福もち rice cake with an·ko inside

dai·kon 大根 Chinese radish (giant white radish)

dan·go だんご round balls made from rice & flour

da·shi だし stock, usually made from ka·tsu·o·bu·shi or kom·bu

…·don …丼 rice with savoury topping

do·ra·ya·ki どら焼き sweet a·zu·ki bean paste between two pancakes

~ e ~

e·bi エビ general term for prawn, shrimp, lobster & crayfish

e·bi·fu·rai エビフライ battered prawn

e·bi·sō·men エビそうめん shrimp sō·men

e·da·ma·me 枝豆 young soy bean – a favourite beer snack

e·ki·ben 駅弁 station lunchbox

ē·ru エール ale

~ f ~

fu·e·dai フエダイ snapper

fu·gu フグ puffer(fish) • globefish

fu·ri·ka·ke ふりかけ dried topping for rice

fu·rū·tsu·jū·su フルーツジュース fruit juice

fu·to·ma·ki 太巻き various ingredients rolled in no·ri seaweed (large sushi rolls)

~ g ~

gem·mai 玄米 brown rice

gem·mai·cha 玄米茶 roasted tea

go·han ご飯 cooked rice • general term for 'a meal'

go·ma ごま sesame seeds

go·ma·dō·fu ごま豆腐 tō·fu-like food made of ground white sesame & starch

gu·rē·pu·fu·rū·tsu グレープフルーツ grapefruit

gyō·za ギョウザ Chinese-style dumplings, normally made from minced pork, cabbage, garlic, ginger & garlic chives

gyū·don 牛丼 thinly sliced beef simmered in sweetened shō·yu & served on rice

gyū·ni·ku 牛肉 beef

gyū·nyū 牛乳 milk

gyū·tan 牛タン beef tongue

~ *h* ~

hā·bu·tī ハーブティー herbal tea

ha·ma·gu·ri ハマグリ clam

ha·mu ハム ham

ha·sa·mi はさみ crab claws

hi·ji·ki ひじき a type of seaweed

hi·ki·ni·ku ひき肉 mince

hi·ra·ta·ke ヒラタケ oyster mushroom

hi·tsu·ji 羊 sheep • lamb

hi·ya·mu·gi 冷麦 cold noodles dipped in cold sauce

hi·ya·shi·u·don 冷やしうどん simple cold u·don

hi·ya·yak·ko 冷奴 cold tō·fu

hok·ke ホッケ atka mackerel

hō·ren·sō ホウレンソウ spinach

ho·so·ma·ki 細まき thin sushi roll

~ *i* ~

i·chi·go イチゴ strawberry

i·gai 貽貝 mussel (also known as mū·ru·gai)

i·ka イカ squid • cuttlefish

i·ku·ra イクラ salted salmon eggs

i·na·ri·zu·shi 稲荷ずし vinegared rice in a fried tō·fu pouch

i·ri·ko いりこ sea cucumber • dried trepang (sea cucumber) • dried sardine

i·se·e·bi イセエビ Japanese spiny lobster • crayfish

...i·ta·me …炒め stir-fried ...

~ *j* ~

ja·ga·ba·tā ジャガバター baked potatoes with butter

ja·ga·i·mo ジャガイモ potatoes

jin·jā ジンジャー ginger

...ji·ru …汁 … juice • … soup

ji·za·ke 地酒 local sa·ke

~ *k* ~

ka·bo·cha かぼちゃ Japanese pumpkin

kai(·ru·i) 貝(類) shellfish

kai·sam·bu·tsu 海産物 seafood

kai·se·ki·ryō·ri 懐石料理 multi-course set meal including many small dishes – also known as kai·se·ki

ka·ki 柿 persimmon

ka·ki カキ oyster

ka·ki·a·ge かき揚げ finely chopped seafood & vegetables fried in tem·pu·ra batter

ka·mo 鴨 duck

ka·ni カニ crab

ka·ra·a·ge から揚げ meat or fish dusted in flour & deep-fried

ka·ra·me·ru カラメル caramel (baked sugar)

ka·rē カレー curry

ka·rē·rai·su カレーライス Japanese-style curry & rice

ka·rē·u·don カレーうどん u·don noodles with curry roux sauce (ie sauce based on equal amounts of fat and flour)

ka·tsu カツ cutlets

ka·tsu·don カツ丼 fried pork cutlet & egg on rice

ka·tsu·o カツオ bonito • skipjack

ka·tsu·o·bu·shi カツオ節 dried bonito (fish) flakes

kē·ki ケーキ cake(s)

ki·i·chi·go キイチゴ raspberry

ki·na·ko きなこ soy bean flour

ki no mi 木の実 berries

ki·no·ko きのこ mushroom

ki·tsu·ne·u·don きつねうどん wheat flour noodles with fried tō·fu

kō·be·gyū 神戸牛 beef from Kobe renowned as marble beef

kō·cha 紅茶 (black) tea

kō·hī コーヒー coffee

ko·hi·tsu·ji 子羊 lamb

ko·ko·a ココア cocoa

kom·bu 昆布 kelp (seaweed)

kon·nya·ku 婚約者 gelatinous paste made from tubers often used in stews, oden and hotpots

ko·shō 胡椒 pepper

ku·da·mo·no くだもの fruit

ku·ji·ra くじら whale

ku·ra·ge クラゲ jellyfish

ku·ri 栗 chestnut

ku·ro·go·ma 黒ごま black sesame seed

kya·be·tsu キャベツ cabbage

kyū·ri キュウリ cucumber

~ m ~

ma·gu·ro マグロ tuna – caught mostly outside Japan

ma·ki·zu·shi 巻きずし general term for no·ri-rolled sushi

ma·me 豆 beans, including pea & soy beans

man·gō マンゴー mango

man·jū 饅頭 steamed bun filled with sweet a·zu·ki beans

44

mat·cha 抹茶 powdered green tea

ma·yo·nē·zu マヨネーズ mayonnaise

me·ron メロン melon

mi·kan みかん mandarin orange

mi·rin みりん sweet rice wine used for cooking

mi·ru·ku ミルク milk

mi·ru·ku·tī ミルクティー milk tea

mi·so 味噌 fermented soy-bean paste – can also be made from rice or barley

mi·so·shi·ru 味噌汁 soup made from mi·so paste with fish stock

mi·zu 水 water

mo·chi もち rice cake made from glutinous rice

mo·mo 桃 peach

mu·gi·cha 麦茶 cold tea made of roasted barley

mu·shi·gyō·za 蒸しギョウザ steamed gyō·za dumpling

mu·shi·mo·no 蒸し物 steamed dishes

~ n ~

…na·be …鍋 hotpot made of …

na·be·ya·ki·u·don 鍋焼きうどん u·don noodles, seafood, meat & vegetables cooked in a small pot

na·ma·ta·ma·go 生卵 raw egg

na·su ナス eggplant • aubergine

ni·ku 肉 meat

ni·ku·dan·go 肉団子 meatball

ni·ku·ja·ga 肉じゃが potato & meat stew

nin·jin ニンジン carrot

nin·ni·ku ニンニク garlic

no·ri 海苔 sea laver • type of seaweed formed into sheets & used to wrap sushi

no·ri·ma·ki 海苔巻 sushi rolled in seaweed

~ o ~

o·cha お茶 Japanese green tea

o·cha·zu·ke お茶漬け white rice with green tea poured onto it

o·den おでん hotpot with tō·fu, kon·nya·ku, fish-cake meatballs & potato stewed in stock

o·ka·shi お菓子 sweets • lollies

o·ko·no·mi·ya·ki お好み焼き Japanese-style savoury pancake

o·mu·rai·su オムライス dish consisting of omelette with a rice filling

o·mu·re·tsu オムレツ omelette

o·ni·gi·ri おにぎり rice ball

o·ren·ji オレンジ orange

…o·ro·shi …おろし grated …

o·sa·ke お酒 Japanese wine

o·ya·ko·don 親子丼 chicken & egg on rice

~ p ~

pā·chi パーチ perch
pan パン bread • bread roll
pan·ko パン粉 breadcrumbs
pas·ta パスタ pasta
pō·ku ポーク pork (also called bu·ta·ni·ku)
pon·zu ポン酢 juice from citrus fruits • a mix of shō·yu, da·shi, citrus juices & sometimes vinegar
po·te·to ポテト potatoes
po·te·to·fu·rai ポテトフライ fried potatoes • French fries

~ r ~

ra·dis·shu ラディッシュ radish
rā·men ラーメン yellow wheat noodles
rā·yu ラー油 chilli oil
re·mon レモン lemon
re·mon·tī レモンティー lemon tea
ren·kon れんこん lotus root
rē·shu 冷酒 chilled sa·ke
rin·go りんご apple

~ s ~

sa·ba サバ chub mackerel • Pacific mackerel
sa·ka·na 魚 fish
sa·ke 酒 alcohol made from a fermenting process that uses grain • general term for alcoholic drinks

(also called o·sa·ke & ni·hon·shu)
sa·ke 鮭 salmon • chum salmon • dog salmon (also known as sha·ke)
sa·ku·ra·mo·chi 桜もち pink rice cake wrapped in a cherry leaf
sa·ku·ram·bo さくらんぼ cherry
sam·ma さんま Pacific saury • saury pike
sa·shi·mi 刺身 raw fish or meat
sa·tō 砂糖 sugar
se·ki·han 赤飯 'red rice' with a·zu·ki beans
sem·bē せんべい rice cracker
sen·cha 煎茶 a typical Japanese green tea
sha·bu·sha·bu しゃぶしゃぶ thinly sliced beef dipped into a boiling hotpot, then into sesame or pon·zu sauces
shi·me·ji しめじ a type of mushroom
shi·mo·fu·ri (gyū·ni·ku) 霜降り (牛肉) marbled (beef)
shi·o 塩 salt
shi·ra·su シラス whitebait
shi·ra·ta·ki しらたき kon·nya·ku in noodle form
shi·ro·go·ma 白ごま white sesame seed
shi·ro·wain 白ワイン white wine
shi·ro·za·ke 白酒 white, cloudy rice wine

shī·ta·ke しいたけ shiitake mushroom

shō·chū 焼酎 distilled spirit made from sweet potato, rice, millet or lees (sediment) from rice wine

shō·ga しょうが ginger

shō·jin·ryō·ri 精進料理 traditional Buddhist vegetarian food

so·ba そば buckwheat • buckwheat noodles

sō·men そうめん fine wheat noodles eaten cold & dipped in sauce

su·i·ka すいか watermelon

su·ki·ya·ki すき焼き beef, tō·fu, vegetables & shi·ra·ta·ki cooked in an iron pan with shō·yu, sugar & sa·ke & served with raw egg dip

sū·pu スープ soup

~ *t* ~

tai タイ snapper • bream

ta·ke·no·ko タケノコ bamboo shoots

ta·ko タコ octopus

ta·ko·ya·ki タコ焼き flour batter balls with octopus inside, fried

ta·ma·go 卵 egg

ta·ma·go·ya·ki 卵焼き Japanese-style fried egg • omelette

ta·ma·ne·gi たまねぎ onion

ta·ta·ki たたき minced raw fish flesh • meat or fish seared on the outside & served sliced

tek·ka·don 鉄火丼 tuna sa·shi·mi on a large bowl of steamed rice

tek·ka·ma·ki 鉄火巻き tuna sushi roll

te·ma·ki·zu·shi 手巻きずし do-it-yourself sushi roll

tem·pu·ra てんぷら seafood, meat & vegetables deep-fried in light batter & eaten dipped in a light sauce

ten·don 天丼 battered prawn on rice

te·ri·ya·ki 照り焼き meat or fish, brushed with marinade of shō·yu, mi·rin & sugar, then grilled

tē·sho·ku 定食 set menu

tō·fu とうふ soy-bean curd

tō·ga·ra·shi とうがらし red chilli pepper • cayenne

ton·ko·tsu·rā·men とんこつラーメン rā·men with white pork broth

to·ri·ni·ku 鶏肉 chicken (meat)

to·ro とろ the fattiest (and also considered the tastiest) meat of tuna fish ma·gu·ro

tsu·ku·ne つくね minced fish or chicken balls eaten fried or boiled

tsu·mi·re つみれ fish-cake balls – used in o·den & stew

~ *u* ~

u·don うどん thick noodles made of wheat flour

u·me 梅 Japanese plum
u·me·bo·shi 梅干 dried & pickled Japanese plum
u·na·don うな丼 grilled eel on rice
u·na·gi うなぎ eel
u·ni ウニ sea urchin
ū·ron·cha 烏龍茶 oolong tea

~ w ~

wa·ga·shi 和菓子 Japanese sweets
wa·gyū 和牛 Japanese beef
wa·ka·me ワカメ type of seaweed
wa·sa·bi ワサビ very hot Japanese horseradish

~ y ~

…ya …屋 … shop • … restaurant, eg sushi·ya, sha·bu·sha·bu·ya
…ya·ki/ya·ki … …焼き/焼き… food that is grilled, baked, barbecued or pan fried
ya·ki·me·shi 焼き飯 fried rice
ya·ki·mo·chi 焼きもち toasted rice cake
ya·ki·mo·no 焼きもの broiled, grilled or pan-fried dishes

ya·ki·ni·ku 焼肉 cook-it-yourself, Korean-style barbecue
ya·ki·o·ni·gi·ri 焼きおにぎり grilled rice ball
ya·ki·so·ba 焼きそば fried so·ba noodles with vegetables, meat & sauce
ya·ki·to·ri 焼きとり grilled meat on skewers
ya·sai 野菜 vegetables
ya·tsu·ha·shi 八橋 sweet cinnamon-flavoured hard crackers (Kyoto Prefecture)
yō·kan ようかん sweet jelly made of ground a·zu·ki beans
yō·sho·ku 洋食 Japanese versions of Western dishes
yu·dō·fu 湯豆腐 tō·fu boiled in a weak kom·bu broth
yu·zu ゆず a type of citrus fruit

~ z ~

za·ru·so·ba ざるそば cold buckwheat noodles served with no·ri, spring onion & wa·sa·bi
ze·rī ゼリー jelly
zu·wai·ga·ni ズワイガニ red crab • snow crab

Sightseeing

≡ Fast Phrases

May I take a photo?	写真を撮ってもいいですか？ sha·shin o tot·te mo ī des ka
When does the museum open?	博物館 は何時に 開きますか？ ha·ku·bu·tsu·kan wa nan·ji ni a·ki·mas·ka
When's the next tour?	次のツアーはいつですか？ tsu·gi no tsu·a wa i·tsu des ka

Planning

Do you have information on cultural sights?	文化的見どころに ついての案内はありますか？ bun·ka·te·ki mi·do·ko·ro ni tsu·i·te no an·nai wa a·ri·mas ka
Can you recommend any local tourist attractions?	地元の観光スポットを お勧めしますか？ ji·mo·to no kan·kō su·pot·to o o su·su·me shi·mas ka
I have one day/one week.	1日/1週間 あります。 i·chi·ni·chi/i·shū·kan a·ri·mas
I'd like a guide please.	ガイドをお願いします。 gai·do o o·ne·gai shi·mas

| **I'd like to see ...** | …を見ようと思います。 |
| | ... o mi·yō to o·moy·mas |

I'm interested in ...	…に興味が あります。	... ni kyō·mi ga a·ri·mas
temples	寺	te·ra
historic sites	史跡	shi·se·ki
art galleries	美術館	bi·ju·tsu·kan
gardens	庭	ni·wa
local food specialties	当地料理	go·tō·ji ryō·ri
shopping	買い物	kai·mo·no

Questions

What's that?	あれは何ですか?
	a·re wa nan des ka
How old is it?	どのくらい古いですか?
	do·no ku·rai fu·ru·i des ka
Could you please take a photo of me?	私の写真を撮って もらえませんか?
	wa·ta·shi no sha·shin o tot·te mo·ra·e·ma·sen ka
May I take a photo (of you/it)?	(あなた/あれの)写真を撮って もいいですか?
	(a·na·ta/a·re no) sha·shin o tot·te mo ī des ka
I'll send the photo to you.	あなたに写真をお送りします。
	a·na·ta ni sha·shin o ō·ku·ri shi·mas

Say Cheeeeeese!

When taking a picture of your Japanese friends and acquaintances, ensure their attention – and best smiles – with hai, chī·zu (ハイ、チーズ), 'Say cheese!'

PHRASE BUILDER

I'd like a/an...	…をお願いします。	... o o·ne·gai shi·mas
audio set	オーディオセット	ō·di·o·set·to
catalogue	パンフレット	pan·fu·ret·to
guide	ガイド	gai·do
(local) map	(市街)地図	(shi·gai) chi·zu

Getting In

What time does it open?	何時に開きますか? nan·ji ni a·ki·mas ka
What time does it close?	何時に閉まりますか? nan·ji ni shi·ma·ri·mas ka
What's the admission charge?	入場料はいくらですか? nyū·jō·ryō wa i·ku·ra des ka

Fast Talk

Forming Sentences

You don't need to memorise complete sentences; instead, simply use key words to get your meaning across. For example, you might know that i·tsu (いつ) means 'when' in Japanese. So if you've arranged a tour but don't know what time, just ask tsu·ā wa i·tsu? (ツアーはいつ?). Don't worry that you're not getting the whole sentence right – people will understand if you stick to the key words.

PHRASE BUILDER

Is there a discount for ...?	…割引が ありますか?	…wa·ri·bi·ki ga a·ri·mas ka
children	子供	ko·do·mo
families	家族	ka·zo·ku
groups	グループ	gu·rū·pu
older people	高齢者	kō·rē·sha
students	学生	gak·sē

Galleries & Museums

When is the gallery/ museum open?	美術館/ 博物館 は何時に 開きますか? bi·ju·tsu·kan/ ha·ku·bu·tsu·kan wa nan·ji ni a·ki·mas ka
What's in the collection?	所蔵品には何が ありますか? sho·zō·hin ni wa na·ni ga a·ri·mas ka

PHRASE BUILDER

It's a/an ... exhibition	…の展覧会です。	... no ten·ran·kai des
calligraphy	書道	sho·dō
ceramics	陶芸	tō·gē
ink painting	水墨画	su·i·bo·ku·ga
ukiyo-e prints	浮世絵	ya·ma·to·e

I like the works of ...	…の作品が好きです。 ... no sa·ku·hin ga su·ki des
I'm interested in ...	…に興味があります。 ... ni kyō·mi ga a·ri·mas

Tours

PHRASE BUILDER

When's the next (...)?	次の(…)はいつ ですか?	tsu·gi no (...)wa i·tsu des ka
Can you recommend a (...)?	おすすめの(…) はありますか?	o·su·su·me no (...) wa a·ri·mas ka
tour	ツアー	tsu·ā
boat tour	ボートツアー	bō·to tsu·ā
day trip	1日観光	i·chi·ni·chi kan·kō

| How long is the tour? | ツアーにかかる時間はどのくらいですか? tsu·ā ni ka·ka·ru ji·kan wa do·no ku·rai des ka |
| What do I need to bring with me? | 持ちたいものは何ですか? mo·chi·tai mo·no wa nan·des ka? |

SIGHTSEEING

PHRASE BUILDER

Is the ... included?	…は含まれていますか?	...wa fu·ku·ma·re·te i·mas ka
admission charge	入場料	nyū·jō·ryō
food	食事代	sho·ku·ji·dai
transport	交通費	kō·tsū·hi

| I've lost my group. | グループからはぐれました。 gu·rū·pu ka·ra ha·gu·re·mash·ta |

Shopping

⟺ Fast Phrases

Can I look at it?	それを見てもいいですか?	so·re o mi·te mo ī des ka
Can I try it on?	試着できますか?	shi·cha·ku de·ki·mas ka
How much is it?	おいくらですか?	o·i·ku·ra des ka

Looking For...

PHRASE BUILDER

Where's a...?	…はどこですか?	wa do·ko des ka
bank	銀行	gin·kō
department store	デパート	de·pā·to
supermarket	スーパ	sū·pa

Where can I buy locally produced goods/souvenirs?	地元産の製品／お土産は、どこで買えますか? ji·mo·to·san no sē·hin/o·mi·ya·ge wa do·ko de ka·e·mas ka

Shopping Secrets

Where can I buy souvenirs/gifts?	お土産を買う場所は どこですか?	o·mi·ya·ge o kow ba·sho wa do·ko des·ka
Are there any sales?	何かバーゲンは やっていますか?	na·ni ka bā·gen wa yat·tei·mas·ka

In the Shop

I'd like to buy ...	…をください。	... o ku·da·sai
I'm just looking.	見ているだけです。	mi·te i·ru da·ke des
Can I look at it?	それを見てもいい ですか?	so·re o mi·te mo ī des ka
Can I try it on?	試着できますか?	shi·cha·ku de·ki·mas ka
Do you have any others?	ほかに何か ありますか?	ho·ka ni na·ni ka a·ri·mas ka
What is it made from?	何から作られたの ですか?	na·ni ka·ra tsu·ku·ra·re·ta no·des ka?
It's faulty.	不良品です。	fu·ryō·hin des
Could I have it wrapped?	包んで もらえますか?	tsu·tsun·de mo·ra·e·mas ka

SHOPPING

Paying

How much is it?	おいくらですか？ o·i·ku·ra des ka
✂ How much?	おいくら？ o·i·ku·ra
Can you write down the price?	値段を書いてもらえますか？ ne·dan o kai·te mo·ra·e·mas ka
That's too expensive.	高すぎます。 ta·ka·su·gi·mas
Do you have something cheaper?	もっと安いものがありますか？ mot·to ya·su·i mo·no ga a·ri·mas ka
Can you give me a discount?	ディスカウントできますか？ dis·kown·to de·ki·mas ka
I'd like my change please	お釣りをお願いします。 o·tsu·ri o o·ne·gai shi·mas
Do you accept credit cards?	クレジットカードで 支払えますか？ ku·re·jit·to·kā·do de shi·ha·ra·e·mas ka

PHRASE BUILDER

I'd like...	…をください。	... o ku·da·sai
a bag	袋	fu·ku·ro
a receipt	レシート	re·shī·to

I'd like a refund please.	払い戻しをお願い します。 ha·rai·mo·do·shi o o·ne·gai shi·mas

57

Fast Talk

Japanese Souvenirs

Common Japanese souvenirs (o·mi·ya·ge
お土産) and gifts include folding fans (sen·su 扇子), ceramics (tō·gē 陶芸), tea sets (cha·ki 茶器), lacquerware (shik·ki
漆器), handmade paper (wa·shi 和紙) and Japanese dolls
(ni·hon nin·gyō 日本人形). Art lovers will find beautiful
scrolls (ka·ke·ji·ku 掛け軸) and woodblock prints (u·ki·yo·e
浮世絵), samurai enthusiasts can look for Japanese swords
(ka·ta·na 刀), and the cotton kimono (yu·ka·ta 浴衣) is an
ever-popular lightweight souvenir.

I'd like to return this, please.	返品をお願いします。	hem·pin o o·ne·gai shi·mas

Clothes

My size is (L/M/S).	私のサイズは (L/M/S) です。	wa·ta·shi no sai·zu wa (e·ru/e·mu/e·su) des
Can I try it on?	試着 できますか?	shi·cha·ku de·ki·mas ka

PHRASE BUILDER

I'm looking for...	… を探しています。	...o sa·ga·shte·i·mas
shoes	靴	ku·tsu
underwear	下着	shi·ta·gi
swimwear	水着	mi zu gi

It doesn't fit.	体にフィット しません。	ka·ra·da ni fit·to shi·ma·sen

Books & Music

Do you have a book by ...?	… の本は ありますか?	...no hon wa a·ri·mas ka
Is there an English-language section?	英語のセクション はありますか?	ē·go no sek·shon wa a·ri·mas ka
I'd like a dictionary.	辞書をください。	ji·sho o ku·da·sai
I'd like a newspaper (in English).	(英字)新聞を ください。	(ē·ji) shim·bun o ku·da·sai
I'd like a CD/DVD.	CD/DVDを ください。	shī·dī/dī·bī·dī o ku·da·sai
I'm looking for music by ...	… の曲を 探しています。	no kyo·ku o sa·ga·shi·te i·mas
Can I listen to this?	これを聴いても いいですか?	ko·re o kī·te mo ī des ka

Entertainment

≡ Fast Phrases

What's on tonight?	今夜は何がありますか? kon·ya wa na·ni ga a·ri·mas ka
What time shall we meet?	何時に会いましょうか? nan·ji ni ai·ma·shō ka
Where shall we meet?	どこで会いましょうか? do·ko de ai·ma·shō

Going Out

Is there a local entertainment guide?	地元のエンターテイメント ガイドはありますか? ji·mo·to no en·tā·tē·men·to gai·do wa a·ri·mas ka
What's on this weekend?	今週の週末は 何がありますか? kon·shū no shū·ma·tsu wa na·ni ga a·ri·mas ka
What's on today?	今日は何がありますか? kyō wa na·ni ga a·ri·mas ka
Can you recommend a good bar?	いいバーを知っていますか? ī bā o shit·te i·mas ka
Would you like to go for a drink?	飲みに行きませんか? no·mi ni i·ki·ma·sen ka

60

Karaoke

Karaoke boxes (カラオケボックス ka·ra·o·ke·bok·ksu) –
rooms for karaoke that can be booked on an hourly basis
and where you can also be served food and drinks – are
hugely popular in Japan. A few phrases that might come in
handy while out singing: 'Let's sing together' (いっしょに歌
いましょう is·sho ni u·tai·ma·shō), 'Are there English songs?'
(英語の曲がありますか? ē·go no kyo·ku ga a·ri·mas ka), 'I
don't know this song' (この曲は知りません。ko·no kyo·ku
wa shi·ri·ma·sen), and, for when you'd rather just watch, 'I'm
not good at singing' (歌うのが上手じゃありません u·ta·u no
ga jō·zu ja a·ri·ma·sen).

PHRASE BUILDER

Where can I find ...?	どこに行けば…がありますか?	do·ko ni i·ke·ba ... ga a·ri·mas ka
clubs	クラブ	ku·ra·bu
gay venues	ゲイの場所	gē no ba·sho
Japanese-style pubs	居酒屋	i·za·ka·ya
places to eat	食事ができる所	sho·ku·ji ga de·ki·ru to·ko·ro

PHRASE BUILDER

I feel like going to a ...	…に行きたい気分です。	... ni i·ki·tai ki·bun des
ballet	バレエ	ba·rē
bar	バー	bā
cafe	カフェ	ka·fe
live band	ライブ	rai·bu
film	映画	ē·ga
karaoke	カラオケ	ka·ra·o·ke
play	劇	ge·ki
restaurant	レストラン	res·to·ran

Meeting Up

What time shall we meet?	何時に会いましょうか? nan·ji ni ai·ma·shō ka
Where shall we meet?	どこで会いましょうか? doko de ai·ma·shō ka
Let's meet at (eight) o'clock.	(8)時に会いましょう。 (ha·chi)·ji ni ai·ma·shō
Let's meet at (the entrance).	(入口)で会いましょう。 (i·ri·gu·chi) de ai·ma·shō
See you tomorrow.	明日会いましょう。 a·shi·ta ai·ma·shō
I'm looking forward to it.	楽しみにしています。 ta·no·shi·mi ni shi·te i·mas
Sorry I'm late.	遅れてすみません。 o·ku·re·te su·mi·ma·sen
OK!	OK! ō·kē

Practicalities

Fast Phrases

Is there Wi-Fi here?	ここにWi-Fiがありますか? ko·ko ni wai·fai ga a·ri·mas·ka?
Where's an ATM?	ATMはどこですか? ē·tī·e·mu wa do·ko des ka
Where are the toilets?	トイレはどこですか? toy·re wa do·ko des ka

Bank

I'd like to ...	…をお願い します。 ... o o·ne·gai shi·mas
Where can I ...?	どこで…できますか? do·ko de ... de·ki·mas ka
change money	両替 ryō·ga·e
Where's an ATM?	ATMはどこですか? ē·tī·e·mu wa do·ko des ka
Where's a foreign exchange counter?	外国為替の 窓口はどこですか? gai·ko·ku·ka·wa·se no ma·do·gu·chi wa do·ko des ka
What's the exchange rate?	為替レートはいくらですか? ka·wa·se·rē·to wa i·ku·ra des ka

What's the charge?	料金はいくらですか？	ryō·kin wa i·ku·ra des ka
What time does the bank open?	銀行は何時に開きますか？	gin·kō wa nan·ji ni hi·ra·ki·mas ka

Phone

PHRASE BUILDER

I'd like a ...	…をお願いします。	... o o·ne·gai shi·mas
charger for my phone	携帯電話の充電器	kē·tai·den·wa no jū·den·ki
prepaid SIM card	プリペイドシム	pu·ri·pē·do shim u
data SIM card	データシム	dē ta shim u

Internet

Is there wi-fi here?	ここにWi-Fiがありますか？	wi-fi ga a·ri·mas·ka?
What is the wi-fi password?	Wi-Fiのパスワードは何ですか？	wi-fi no pa·su·wā·do wa nan·des·ka?
Can I connect my laptop here?	私のノートパソコンに接続してもいいですか？	wa·ta·shi no nō·to·pa·so·kon ni se·tsu·zo·ku shi·te mo ī des ka
Where's an internet cafe?	インターネットカフェはどこですか？	in·tā·net·to·ka·fe wa do·ko des ka

I'd like to use Skype	スカイプを使いたいのですが。
	skaip o tsu·kai·tai no des ga

PHRASE BUILDER

I'd like to ...	…したいのですが。	... shi·tai no des ga
check my email	Eメールをチェック	ī·mē·ru o chek·ku
use a printer	プリント	prin·to

How much per hour?	1時間いくらですか?
	i·chi·ji·kan i·ku·ra des ka
How much per (five) minutes?	(5)分間いくらですか?
	(go)·fun·kan i·ku·ra des ka
Please change it to the English-language setting	英語のセッティングにしてください。
	ē·go no set·tin·gu ni shi·te ku·da·sai

PRACTICALITIES

Fast Talk

Understanding Japanese

Most sentences are composed of several words (or parts of words) serving various grammatical functions, as well as those that carry meaning (primarily nouns and verbs). If you're finding it hard to understand what someone is saying to you, listen out for the nouns and verbs to work out the context – this shouldn't be hard as they are usually more emphasised in speech. If you're still having trouble, a useful phrase to know is もっとゆっくり 話してくれませんか? mot·to yuk·ku·ri ha·na·shi·te ku·re·ma·sen ka (Please speak more slowly).

Emergencies

PHRASE BUILDER

Call ...	を呼んで。	o yon·de
the police	警察	kē·sa·tsu
a doctor	医者	i·sha
an ambulance	救急車	kyū·kyū·sha

Help!	たすけて!	tas·ke·te
Stop!	止まれ!	to·ma·re
Go away!	離れろ!	ha·na·re·ro
Thief!	どろぼう!	do·ro·bō
Fire!	火事だ!	ka·ji da
Watch out!	危ない!	a·bu·nai
It's an emergency.	緊急です。	kin·kyū des

PHRASE BUILDER

I've lost my ...	…をなくしました。	... o na·ku·shi·mash·ta
bags	バッグ	bag·gu
money	お金	o·ka·ne
wallet	財布	sai·fu
passport	パスポート	pas·pō·to

66

Could you please help?	たすけてください。	tas·ke·te ku·da·sai
Can I use your phone?	電話を貸してくれませんか？	den·wa o ka·shi·te ku·re·ma·sen ka
Where are the toilets?	トイレはどこですか？	toy·re wa do·ko des ka

PHRASE BUILDER

Where's the nearest ...?	この近くの… はどこですか？	ko·no chi·ka·ku no ... wa do·ko des ka
hospital	病院	byō·in
chemist	薬局	yak·kyo·ku
dentist	歯医者	ha·i·sha

I'm lost.	道に迷いました。	mi·chi ni ma·yoy·mash·ta

Police

Where's the police station?	警察署はどこですか？	kē·sa·tsu·sho wa do·ko des ka
I've been robbed.	私は強盗に遭いました	wa·ta·shi wa gō·tō ni ai·mash·ta
I've been raped.	私はレイプされました	wa·ta·shi wa rē·pu sa·re·mash·ta
I want to contact my embassy/consulate	領事館/大使館に連絡 したいです	ryō·ji·kan/tai·shi·kan ni ren·ra·ku shi·tai des
I have insurance	私は保険を持っている	wa·ta·shi wa ho·ken o mo·tte i·ru

PHRASE BUILDER

I feel ...	私は...	wa·ta·shi wa ...
dizzy	めまいがします	me·mai ga shi·mas
hot and cold	暑くなったり 寒くなったり します	a·tsu·ku nat·ta·ri sa·mu·ku nat·ta·ri shi·mas
nauseated	吐き気がします	ha·ki·ke ga shi·mas
weak	ちからが ありません	chi·ka·ra ga a·ri·ma·sen

I need a doctor (who speaks English).	(英語ができる)お医者さんが 必要です。 (ē·go ga de·ki·ru) oy·sha·san ga hi·tsu·yō des	
Could I see a female doctor?	女性のお医者さんをお願い できますか? jo·sē no oy·sha·san o o·ne·gai de·ki·mas ka	

PHRASE BUILDER

I'm allergic to...	私は… アレルギーです。	wa·ta·shi wa ... a·re·ru·gī des
antibiotics	抗生物質	kō·sē·bus·shi·tsu
aspirin	アスピリン	as·pi·rin
penicillin	ペニシリン	pe·ni·shi·rin

Symptoms & Allergies

I'm sick.	私は病気です。 wa·ta·shi wa byō·ki des
It hurts here.	ここが痛いです。 ko·ko ga i·tai des
I've been injured.	私はけがをしました。 wa·ta·shi wa ke·ga o shi·mash·ta
I've been vomiting.	私はもどしています。 wa·ta·shi wa mo·do·shi·te i·mas
I have a cold	風邪をひきました。 ka·ze ohi·ki·mash·ta
I have a toothache	歯が痛いです。 ha ga i·tai des

PHRASE BUILDER

I have (...)	私は…があります。	wa·ta·shi wa ... ga a·ri·mas
asthma	喘息	zen·so·ku
diarrhoea	下痢	ge·ri
headache	頭痛	zu·tsū
fever	熱	ne·tsu

I'm on medication for ...	…の薬を飲んでいます。 ... no ku·su·ri o non·de i·mas
I need something for (a headache).	なにか(頭痛)に効くもの が必要です。 na·ni ka (zu·tsū) ni ki·ku·mo·no ga hi·tsu·yō des

Dictionary

ENGLISH *to* JAPANESE

英語 – 日本語

Verbs in this dictionary are in their ·mas (ます) form (for more information on this, see p5). The symbols ⓝ, ⓐ and ⓥ (indicating noun, adjective and verb) have been added for clarity where an English term could be either. Basic food terms have been included – for a more extensive list of ingredients and dishes, see the menu decoder (p41).

- a -

accommodation 宿泊 shu·ku·ha·ku
adaptor アダプター a·da·pu·tā
admission (price) 入場料 nyū·jō·ryō
adult ⓝ 大人 o·to·na
aeroplane 飛行機 hi·kō·ki
after あと a·to
afternoon 午後 go·go
ahead 向うに mu·kō ni
air-conditioning エアコン air·kon
airport 空港 kū·kō
alcohol アルコール a·ru·kō·ru
alcove (in house) 床の間 to·ko·no·ma
all 全部 zem·bu
allergy アレルギー a·re·ru·gī
antihistamines 抗ヒスタミン剤 kō·hi·su·ta·min·zai

antique ⓝ アンティーク an·tī·ku
antiseptic ⓝ 消毒剤 shō·do·ku·zai
appointment 予約 yo·ya·ku
arrivals 到着 tō·cha·ku
art 美術 bi·ju·tsu
autumn 秋 a·ki

- b -

baby 赤ちゃん a·ka·chan
baby food 離乳食 ri·nyū·sho·ku
back (body part) 背中 se·na·ka
bag (general) かばん ka·ban
bag (shopping) 袋 fu·ku·ro
baggage 手荷物 te·ni·mo·tsu
baggage allowance 手荷物許容量 te·ni·mo·tsu·kyo·yō·ryō
bakery パン屋 pan·ya

bandage 包帯 hō·tai

bar バー bā

bath ⓝ お風呂 o·fu·ro

bath house 銭湯 sen·tō

beautiful 美しい u·tsu·ku·shī

bed ベッド bed·do

best 最高の sai·kō no

bet ⓝ 賭け ka·ke

bicycle 自転車 ji·ten·sha

big 大きい ō·kī

bike 自転車 ji·ten·sha

bill (restaurant etc) ⓝ 勘定 kan·jō

bird 鳥 to·ri

birthday 誕生日 tan·jō·bi

bite (insect) ⓝ 虫刺され
mu·shi·sa·sa·re

black 黒い ku·roy

black (coffee) ブラック bu·rak·ku

blanket 毛布 mō·fu

blood 血 chi

blood pressure 血圧 ke·tsu·a·tsu

blue 青い a·oy

board (a plane, ship etc) ⓥ 乗ります
no·ri·mas

boarding pass 搭乗券 tō·jō·ken

boat ⓝ 船 fu·ne

body 体 ka·ra·da

bone 骨 ho·ne

book ⓝ 本 hon

booked out 満席 man·se·ki

bookshop 本屋 hon·ya

boots (footwear) ブーツ bū·tsu

bottle (alchohol) shop 酒屋 sa·ka·ya

bowl ⓝ ボール bō·ru

bra ブラジャー bu·ra·jā

bread パン pan

breakfast 朝食・朝ごはん chō·sho·ku
· a·sa·go·han

broken 壊れた ko·wa·re·ta

brother 兄弟 kyō·dai

bullet train 新幹線 shin·kan·sen

bus (city) (市)バス (shi) bas

business man サラリーマン
sa·ra·rī·man

buy ⓥ 買います kai·mas

~ c ~

cafe カフェ ka·fe

calligraphy 書道 sho·dō

camera カメラ ka·me·ra

can (be able) できます de·ki·mas

cancel キャンセル kyan·se·ru

car 自動車 ji·dō·sha

carry 運びます ha·ko·bi·mas

carry-on luggage 機内持込の手荷物
ki·nai·mo·chi·ko·mi no te·ni·mo·tsu

cash 現金 gen·kin

cashier レジ re·ji

castle 城 shi·ro

cave 洞窟 dō·ku·tsu

celebration お祝い oy·wai

cell phone 携帯電話 kē·tai·den·wa

cemetery 墓地 bo·chi

centimetre センチ sen·chi

ceramics セラミックス
se·ra·mik·ku·su

chair 椅子 i·su

changing room (in shop) 試着室
shi·cha·ku·shi·tsu

cheap 安い ya·su·i

check-in (desk) ⓝ チェックイン
chek·ku·in

chemist (shop) 薬局 yak·kyo·ku

cherry blossom 桜 sa·ku·ra

chest (body) 胸 mu·ne

child 子供 ko·do·mo

choose 選びます e·ra·bi·mas

chopsticks はし ha·shi

cigarette タバコ ta·ba·ko

cinema 映画館 ē·ga·kan

clean ⓐ きれいな ki·rē na

clock 時計 to·kē

clothes 衣類 i·ru·i

cloudy 曇りの ku·mo·ri·no

colour 色 i·ro
complaint 苦情 ku·jō
complimentary (free) 無料 mu·ryō
condom コンドーム kon·dō·mu
consulate 領事館 ryō·ji·kan
contact lenses コンタクトレンズ kon·ta·ku·to·ren·zu
contraceptives (devices) 避妊具 hi·nin·gu
contraceptives (medicine) 避妊薬 hi·nin·ya·ku
convenience store コンビニ kom·bi·ni
cool (temperature) 涼しい su·zu·shī
cough medicine せき止め se·ki·do·me
countryside 田舎 i·na·ka
credit card クレジットカード ku·re·jit·to·kā·do
currency exchange 為替 ka·wa·se
cycling ⑩ サイクリング sai·ku·rin·gu

-d-

dangerous 危ない a·bu·nai
dark 暗い ku·rai
date of birth 誕生日 tan·jō·bi
daughter 娘 mu·su·me
dawn 夜明け yo·a·ke
(the) day after tomorrow あさって a·sat·te
day trip 1日観光 i·chi·ni·chi kan·kō
decaffeinated デカフェ de·ka·fe
dentist 歯医者 ha·i·sha
deodorant 消臭剤 shō·shū·zai
department store デパート de·pā·to
departure 出発 shup·pa·tsu
deposit (refundable) 預かり金 a·zu·ka·ri·kin
dessert デザート de·zā·to
diarrhoea 下痢 ge·ri
dictionary 辞書 ji·sho
difficult 難しい mu·zu·ka·shī

dinner 夕食・晩ごはん yū·sho·ku・ban·go·han
direct 直接に cho·ku·se·tsu ni
do します shi·mas
doctor 医者 i·sha
dress ⑩ ドレス do·res
drink ⑩ 飲み物 no·mi·mo·no
drink ⓥ 飲みます no·mi·mas
drug (medicine) 薬 ku·su·ri
drunk ⓐ 酔った yot·ta

-e-

ear 耳 mi·mi
early 早く ha·ya·ku
earplugs 耳栓 mi·mi·sen
earrings イヤリング i·ya·rin·gu
elevator エレベータ e·re·bē·ta
email Eメール ī·mē·ru
embassy 大使館 tai·shi·kan
emergency 救急 kyū·kyū
English 英語 ē·go
enjoy (oneself) 楽しみます ta·no·shi·mi·mas
evening 晩 ban
every 毎 mai
everyone みんな min·na
everything 全部 zem·bu
excess (baggage) 超過 chō·ka
exchange rate 為替レート ka·wa·se·rē·to
exhibition 展覧会 ten·ran·kai
exit ⑩ 出口 de·gu·chi
expensive 高い ta·kai
eye 目 me
eye drops 目薬 me·gu·su·ri

-f-

face ⑩ 顔 ka·o
fall (autumn) ⑩ 秋 a·ki
fall (down) ⓥ 倒れます tow·re·mas
family 家族 ka·zo·ku

72

fare 料金 ryō·kin
father お父さん o·tō·san
female 女性 jo·sē
festival 祭 ma·tsu·ri
fever 熱 ne·tsu
finger 指 yu·bi
finish ⓝ 終わり o·wa·ri
fire 火 hi
first-aid kit 救急箱 kyū·kyū·ba·ko
first name 名前 na·ma·e
florist 花屋 ha·na·ya
flower 花 ha·na
food 食べ物 ta·be·mo·no
food poisoning 食中毒
sho·ku·chū·do·ku
forest 森 mo·ri
fragile 壊れやすい ko·wa·re·ya·su·i
friend 友達 to·mo·da·chi
frost 霜 shi·mo
full いっぱい ip·pai
fun ⓐ 楽しい ta·no·shī

-g-

garbage ごみ go·mi
garbage can ごみ箱 go·mi·ba·ko
garden 庭 ni·wa
gas (petrol) ガソリン ga·so·rin
gate (airport, etc) ゲート gē·to
gay (homosexual) ⓝ ゲイの gē·no
gift 贈物 o·ku·ri·mo·no
girl 女の子 on·na·no·ko
girlfriend ガールフレンド
gā·ru·fu·ren·do
glasses (spectacles) 眼鏡 me·ga·ne
gloves 手袋 te·bu·ku·ro
go 行きます i·ki·mas
go out 出かけます de·ka·ke·mas
good いいⅠ
grave 墓 ha·ka
great (fantastic) 素晴らしい
su·ba·ra·shī
green 緑の mi·do·ri no

grey 灰色の hai·ro no
grilled グリルして gu·ri·ru shi·te
guide (information) ⓝ 案内 an·nai
guide (person) ⓝ ガイド gai·do
gym (place) ジム ji·mu

-h-

hair 毛 ke
hairdresser 美容師 bi·yō·shi
halal ハラルの ha·ra·ru no
hand 手 te
handbag ハンドバッグ han·do·bag·gu
harbour 港 mi·na·to
hat 帽子 bō·shi
he 彼は ka·re wa
head 頭 a·ta·ma
headache 頭痛 zu·tsū
heart 心臓 shin·zō
heart attack 心臓麻痺 shin·zō·ma·hi
heart condition 心臓病 shin·zō·byō
heat 熱 ne·tsu
heavy 重い o·moy
help ⓝ たすけ tas·ke
her (ownership) 彼女の ka·no·jo no
her (object of sentence) 彼女を
ka·no·jo o
here ここ ko·ko
hiking ⓝ ハイキング hai·kin·gu
hill 丘 o·ka
him 彼を ka·re o
his 彼の ka·re no
homosexual ⓝ ホモ ho·mo
hospital 病院 byō·in
hot 熱い a·tsu·i
hot spring 温泉 on·sen
hot water お湯 o·yu
hotel ホテル ho·te·ru
how much (money) いくら i·ku·ra
hungry (to be) ⓐ お腹がすいた
o·na·ka ga su·i·ta
hurt ⓥ 傷つけます ki·zu·tsu·ke·mas
husband 夫 ot·to

-i-

I 私は wa·ta·shi wa
ice 氷 kō·ri
ill 病気の byō·ki no
inflammation 発火 hak·ka
influenza インフルエンザ in·fu·ru·en·za
information 情報 jō·hō
injury けが ke·ga
inn (traditional Japanese) 旅館 ryo·kan
insect 虫 mu·shi
inside 内部 nai·bu
interesting おもしろい o·mo·shi·roy
internet インターネット in·tā·net·to
island 島 shi·ma

-j-

jacket ジャケット ja·ket·to
jet lag 時差ぼけ ji·sa·bo·ke
jogging ⓝ ジョギング jo·gin·gu
jumper (sweater) セーター sē·tā

-k-

key 鍵 ka·gi
kilo(gram) キロ (グラム) ki·ro(·gu·ra·mu)
kilometre キロメートル ki·ro·mē·to·ru
kitchen 台所 dai·do·ko·ro
knee ひざ hi·za

-l-

lake 湖 mi·zū·mi
laquerware 漆器 shik·ki
large 大きい ō·kī
last (final) 最後の sai·go no
late 遅い o·soy
later あとで a·to de

launderette コインランドリー
ko·in·ran·do·rī
learn 習います na·rai·mas
leather 皮 ka·wa
left (direction) ⓐ 左 hi·da·ri
left luggage (office) 手荷物預かり所 te·ni·mo·tsu·a·zu·ka·ri·sho
lesbian ⓝ レズ re·zu
less 少ない su·ku·nai
life boat 救命艇 kyū·mē·tē
life jacket 救命胴衣 kyū·mē·dōy
lift (elevator) エレベータ e·re·bē·ta
light ⓝ 電気 den·ki
light (not heavy) 軽い ka·ru·i
lighter (cigarette) ライター rai·tā
like ⓥ 好きです su·ki des
litre リットル rit·to·ru
little (not much) ⓐ 少し su·ko·shi
local ⓐ 地元 ji·mo·to
look ⓥ 見ます mi·mas
look for 探します sa·ga·shi·mas
lost (item) なくした na·ku·shi·ta
lost property office 遺失物取扱所 i·sh i·tsu·bu·tsu·to·ri·a·tsu·kai·jo
luggage 手荷物 te·ni·mo·tsu
luggage lockers ロッカー rok·kā
lunch 昼食・昼ごはん chū·sho·ku • hi·ru·go·han

-m-

magazine 雑誌 zas·shi
make ⓥ 作ります tsu·ku·ri·mas
make-up メーキャップ mē·kyap·pu
many たくさんの ta·ku·san no
map 地図 chi·zu
market ⓝ 市場 i·chi·ba
maybe たぶん ta·bun
me 私を wa·ta·shi o
meal 食事 sho·ku·ji
meet 会います ai·mas
menu メニュー me·nyū
metre メートル mē·to·ru
midday 正午 shō·go

midnight 真夜中 ma·yo·na·ka
migraine 偏頭痛 hen·zu·tsū
million 百 hya·ku·man
minute 分 fun
mirror ⓝ 鏡 ka·ga·mi
mistake 間違い ma·chi·gai
money お金 o·ka·ne
month 月 ga·tsu
moon 月 tsu·ki
more もっと mot·to
morning 朝 a·sa
morning sickness つわり tsu·wa·ri
mother お母さん o·kā·san
mountain 山 ya·ma
mouth 口 ku·chi
movie 映画 ē·ga
Mr/Mrs/Ms/Miss さん ·san
mum お母さん o·kā·san
muscle 筋肉 kin·ni·ku
museum 博物館 ha·ku·bu·tsu·kan
music 音楽 on·ga·ku
my 私の wa·ta·shi no

- n -

name 名前 na·ma·e
nappy オムツ o·mu·tsu
national park 国立公園
ko·ku·ri·tsu·kō·en
nationality 国籍 ko·ku·se·ki
nature 自然 shi·zen
nausea 吐き気 ha·ki·ke
near 近く chi·ka·ku
neck 首 ku·bi
new 新しい a·ta·ra·shī
next つぎ tsu·gi
next to となり to·na·ri
night 夜 yo·ru
nonsmoking 禁煙の kin·en no
noon (lunchtime) 昼 hi·ru
north 北 ki·ta
nose 鼻 ha·na
not ない nai
nothing 何もない na·ni·mo nai

not yet まだ ma·da
now 今 i·ma

- o -

ocean 海 u·mi
on time 時間どおり ji·kan·dō·ri
one 1 i·chi
one-way (ticket) 片道(切符)
ka·ta·mi·chi(·kip·pu)
open 開いている hi·rai·te i·ru
open ⓥ 開きます hi·ra·ki·mas
open-air baths 露天風呂 ro·tem·bu·ro
opening hours 開店時間 kai·ten·ji·kan
orange (colour) オレンジ o·ren·ji
our 私たちの wa·ta·shi·ta·chi no
overseas 海外 kai·gai

- p -

pacemaker ペースメーカー
pês·mê·kā
pain 痛み i·ta·mi
painkiller 鎮痛剤 chin·tsū·zai
painter 画家 ga·ka
palace 宮殿 kyū·den
pants (trousers) ズボン zu·bon
panty liners 生理用ナプキン
sê·ri·yō·na·pu·kin
pantyhose パンティーストッキング
pan·tî·stok·kin·gu
paper 紙 ka·mi
papers (documents) 書類 sho·ru·i
parents 両親 ryō·shin
park ⓝ 公園 kō·en
park (a car) ⓥ 駐車します chū·sha
shi·mas
partner (intimate) パートナー
pā·to·nā
passport パスポート pas·pō·to
past ⓝ 過去 ka·ko
pay ⓥ 支払います shi·ha·rai·mas
payment 支払い shi·ha·rai

penis ペニス pe·nis
penicillin ペニシリン pe·ni·shi·rin
perfume 香水 kō·su·i
period (menstruation) 月経 gek·kē
period pain 生理痛 sē·ri·tsū
permission 許可 kyo·ka
permit 許可証 kyo·ka·shō
person 人 hi·to
personal 個人的な ko·jin·te·ki na
pharmacy 薬局 yak·kyo·ku
photo 写真 sha·shin
picnic ピクニック pi·ku·nik·ku
pillow 枕 ma·ku·ra
place 場所 ba·sho
plant ⓝ 植物 sho·ku·bu·tsu
plate (big) 皿 sa·ra
plate (small) 小皿 ko·za·ra
platform プラットフォーム
pu·rat·to·fō·mu
pocket ポケット po·ket·to
poisonous 毒の do·ku no
police 警察 kē·sa·tsu
police box 交番 kō·ban
police officer 警官 kē·kan
police station 警察署 kē·sa·tsu·sho
pool (swimming) プール pū·ru
post office 郵便局 yū·bin·kyo·ku
pregnancy test kit 妊娠テストキット
nin·shin·tes·to·kit·to
pregnant 妊娠している nin·shin
shi·te i·ru
prescription 処方箋 sho·hō·sen
pretty かわいい ka·wa·ī
price 値段 ne·dan
pub (bar) パブ pa·bu
public baths 銭湯 sen·tō
public gardens 公園 kō·en
public toilet 公衆トイレ kō·shū·toy·re
pull 引きます hi·ki·mas
purple 紫の mu·ra·sa·ki no
purse 財布 sai·fu
push ⓥ 押します o·shi·mas

~q~

quarter ⓝ 4分の1 yon·bun no i·chi
question ⓝ 質問 shi·tsu·mon
queue ⓝ 列 re·tsu
quick すばやい su·ba·yai
quiet 静かな shi·zu·ka na

~r~

railway station 駅 e·ki
rain ⓝ 雨 a·me
raincoat レインコート re·in·kō·to
rape ⓥ レイプ rê·pu
rash 発疹 has·shin
raw 生の na·ma no
razor 剃刀 ka·mi·so·ri
razor blade 剃刀の刃 ka·mi·so·ri no ha
ready 準備ができた jum·bi ga de·ki·ta
reason ⓝ 理由 ri·yū
receipt レシート re·shī·to
recently 最近 sai·kin
recommend 勧めます su·su·me·mas
red 赤い a·kai
refrigerator 冷蔵庫 rē·zō·ko
relationship 関係 kan·kē
reservation (booking) 予約 yo·ya·ku
rest ⓥ 休みます ya·su·mi·mas
restaurant レストラン res·to·ran
return (come back) ⓥ もどります
mo·do·ri·mas
return ticket 往復切符 ō·fu·ku·kip·pu
right (direction) 右 mi·gi
ring (on finger) ⓝ 指 yu·bi·wa
river 川 ka·wa
road 道 mi·chi
road map ロードマップ rō·do·map·pu
rock 岩 i·wa
room 部屋 he·ya
rope ロープ rō·pu
rubbish ごみ go·mi
ruins 廃墟 hai·kyo
run ⓥ 走ります ha·shi·ri·mas

~ s ~

salad サラダ sa·ra·da
sale セール sē·ru
same 同じ o·na·ji
scarf スカーフ skā·fu
school 学校 gak·kō
sea 海 u·mi
seasick 船酔い fu·na·yoy
season 季節 ki·se·tsu
seat (place) 席 se·ki
see 見ます mi·mas
sex セックス sek·kus
shadow 影 ka·ge
shampoo ⓝ シャンプー sham·pū
shave ⓝ シェービング shē·bin·gu
she 彼女は ka·no·jo wa
sheet (bed) シーツ shī·tsu
shirt シャツ sha·tsu
shoe 靴 ku·tsu
shop ⓝ 店 mi·se
shopping 買い物 kai·mo·no
short (height) 低い hi·ku·i
short (length) 短い mi·ji·kai
shoulder 肩 ka·ta
shower シャワー sha·wā
shrine 神社 jin·ja
sick 病気の byō·ki no
signature サイン sain
silk ⓝ 絹 ki·nu
silver ⓝ 銀 gin
sister 姉妹 shi·mai
sit 座ります su·wa·ri·mas
size (general) サイズ sai·zu
skim milk スキムミルク ski·mu·mi·ru·ku
skin 皮膚 hi·fu
skirt スカート skā·to
sleeping pills 睡眠薬 su·i·min·ya·ku
sleepy 眠い ne·mu·i
slow 遅い o·soy
slowly ゆっくり yuk·ku·ri
small 小さい chī·sai
smell ⓝ におい ni·oy

snow 雪 yu·ki
snow pea サヤエンドウ sa·ya·en·dō
socks 靴下 ku·tsu·shi·ta
someone 誰か da·re ka
something 何か na·ni ka
sometimes ときどき to·ki·do·ki
son 息子 mu·su·ko
soon すぐに su·gu ni
south 南 mi·na·mi
souvenir お土産 o·mi·ya·ge
special ⓐ 特別な to·ku·be·tsu na
spring (season) 春 ha·ru
stairway 階段 kai·dan
station 駅 e·ki
statue 像 zō
stomach 胃 i
stomachache 腹痛 fu·ku·tsū
storm 嵐 a·ra·shi
straight まっすぐな mas·su·gu na
street 道 mi·chi
student 生徒 sē·to
subway/metro 地下鉄 chi·ka·te·tsu
summer 夏 na·tsu
sun 太陽 tai·yō
sunburn 日焼け hi·ya·ke
sunglasses サングラス san·gu·ras
sunny 晴れた ha·re·ta
sunrise 日の出 hi·no·de
sunscreen 日焼け止め hi·ya·ke·do·me
sunset 日の入り hi·no·i·ri
supermarket スーパー sū·pā
surfing ⓝ サーフィン sā·fin
surname 名字 myō·ji
swelling 腫れ ha·re
swim ⓥ 泳ぎます o·yo·gi·mas
swimsuit 水着 mi·zu·gi

~ t ~

table テーブル tē·bu·ru
take a photo 写真を撮ります sha·shin o to·ri·mas
tall 高い ta·kai
tampon タンポン tam·pon

77

tattoo 刺青 i·re·zu·mi
tea ceremony 茶道 sa·dō
teeth 歯 ha
temperature (weather) 気温 ki·on
temple 寺 te·ra
there そこに so·ko ni
think 思います o·moy·mas
thirsty ⓐ のどが渇い no·do ga ka·wai·ta
this month 今月 kon·ge·tsu
this week 今週 kon·shū
this year 今年 ko·to·shi
throat のど no·do
ticket 切符 kip·pu
ticket office 切符売り場 kip·pu·u·ri·ba
time 時間 ji·kan
tired 疲れた tsu·ka·re·ta
to へ e
today 今日 kyō
together いっしょに is·sho ni
toilet トイレ toy·re
tomorrow 明日 a·shi·ta
tonight 今夜 kon·ya
too (expensive etc) すぎる su·gi·ru
toothache 歯痛 ha·i·ta
toothbrush 歯ブラシ ha·bu·ra·shi
toothpaste 練り歯磨き ne·ri·ha·mi·ga·ki
tour ⓝ ツアー tsu·ā
tourist office 観光案内所 kan·kō·an·nai·jo
towel タオル tow·ru
trail ⓝ 足跡 a·shi·a·to
train 電車 den·sha
train station 駅 e·ki
transfer ⓝ 乗り換え no·ri·ka·e
travel ⓥ 旅行します ryo·kō shi·mas
travel sickness 乗り物酔 no·ri·mo·no·yoy

~ u ~

umbrella かさ ka·sa
understand 分かります wa·ka·ri·mas
underwear 下着 shi·ta·gi
university 大学 dai·ga·ku
unusual 珍しい me·zu·ra·shī
useful 便利な ben·ri na

~ v ~

vagina ヴァギナ va·gi·na
valley 谷 ta·ni
valuable ⓐ 高価な kō·ka na
valuables 貴重品 ki·chō·hin
value (price) ⓝ 価値 ka·chi
vegan 厳格な菜食主義者 gen·ka·ku na sai·sho·ku·shu·gi·sha
vegetable(s) 野菜 ya·sai
vegetarian ベジタリアン be·ji·ta·ri·an
very とても to·te·mo
view ⓝ 眺め na·ga·me
village 村 mu·ra
visa ビザ bi·za

~ w ~

wake (someone) up ⓥ 起こします o·ko·shi·mas
wait (for) 待ちます ma·chi·mas
walk 歩きます a·ru·ki·mas
wallet 財布 sai·fu
wall 壁 ka·be
want ⓥ 欲しいです ho·shī des
warm あたたかい a·ta·ta·kai
wash (oneself/something) 洗います a·rai·mas
watch ⓝ 腕時計 u·de·do·kē
water 水 mi·zu

water bottle 水筒 su·i·tō
waterfall 滝 ta·ki
we 私たちは wa·ta·shi·ta·chi wa
weather 天気 ten·ki
weekend 週末 shū·ma·tsu
west 西 ni·shi
what なに na·ni
when いつ i·tsu
where どこ do·ko
which どちら do·chi·ra
white 白い shi·roy
who だれ da·re
why なぜ na·ze
wife 妻 tsu·ma
wind 風 ka·ze
window 窓 ma·do
winter 冬 fu·yu

woman 女性 jo·sē
wrist 手首 te·ku·bi
write 書きます ka·ki·mas

~ y ~

year 年 nen • toshi
yellow 黄色い kī·roy
yes はい haī
yesterday きのう ki·nō
you sg あなた a·na·ta
you pl あなたたち a·na·ta·ta·chi
your あなたの a·na·ta no

~ z ~

zoo 動物園 dō·bu·tsu·en

Dictionary

JAPANESE *to* ENGLISH

The entries in this Japanese–English dictionary are ordered according to the gojūon (or aiueo) system, which is widely used in Japan. The order is: **a**-i-u-e-o-**ka**-ga-ki-gi-kya-gya-kyu-gyu-kyo-gyo-ku-gu-ke-ge-ko-go-**sa**-za-shiji-sha-ja-shu-ju-sho-jo-su-zu-se-ze-so-zo-**ta**-da-chi-(ji)-cha-chu-cho-tsu-(zu)-te-de-to-do-**na**-ni-nya-nyu-nyo-nu-ne-no-**ha**-ba-pa-hi-bi-pi-hya-bya-pya-hyubyu-pyu-hyo-byo-pyo-fu-bu-pu-he-be-pe-ho-bo-po-**ma**-mi-mya-myu-myomu-me-mo-**ya**-yu-yo-**ra**-ri-rya-ryu-ryo-ru-re-ro-**wa-n**

あ *a*

愛 ai love Ⓝ
愛します ai shi·mas love Ⓥ
アイスクリーム ais·ku·rī·mu ice cream
空いている ai·te i·ru vacant
青い a·oy blue
赤い a·kai red
赤ちゃん a·ka·chan baby
赤ワイン a·ka·wain red wine
秋 a·ki autumn • fall
朝 a·sa morning
朝ごはん a·sa·go·han breakfast
あさって a·sat·te (the) day after tomorrow
足 a·shi foot
脚 a·shi leg (body part)
足首 a·shi·ku·bi ankle
明日 a·shi·ta tomorrow

明日の朝 a·shi·ta no a·sa tomorrow morning
明日の午後 a·shi·ta no go·go tomorrow afternoon
明日の夜 a·shi·ta no yo·ru tomorrow evening
あたたかい a·ta·ta·kai warm
頭 a·ta·ma head Ⓝ
新しい a·ta·ra·shī new
熱い a·tsu·i hot
あと a·to after
あなた a·na·ta you sg
あなたたち a·na·ta·ta·chi you pl
危ない a·bu·nai dangerous
甘い a·mai sweet Ⓐ
雨 a·me rain
歩きます a·ru·ki·mas walk
アルコール a·ru·kō·ru alcohol
アレルギー a·re·ru·gī allergy

80

いい ī good
いいえ ī·e no
Eメール ī·mē·ru email ⓝ
行きます i·ki·mas go ⓥ
遺失物取扱所 i·shi·tsu·bu·tsu· to·ri·a·tsu·kai·jo lost property office
医者 i·sha doctor
椅子 i·su chair
1 i·chi one
市場 i·chi·ba market
いつ i·tsu when
いっしょに is·sho ni together
田舎 i·na·ka countryside
今 i·ma now
妹 i·mō·to younger sister
衣類 i·ru·i clothing
色 i·ro colour
インターネット in·tā·net·to internet
インターネットカフェ in·tā·net·to·ka·fe internet cafe
上に u·e ni on • up
うしろ u·shi·ro behind
後ろの u·shi·ro no rear (seat etc) ⓐ
美しい u·tsu·ku·shī beautiful
腕 u·de arm
海 u·mi sea
うるさい u·ru·sai loud • noisy
絵 e painting (a work)
映画 ē·ga film (cinema) • movie
映画館 ē·ga·kan cinema
英語 ē·go English
ATM ē·tī·e·mu automated teller machine (ATM)
駅 e·ki (train) station
エスカレータ es·ka·rē·ta escalator
エレベータ e·re·bē·ta elevator • lift
おいしい oy·shī tasty
往復切符 ō·fu·ku·kip·pu return ticket
大きい ō·kī big
お母さん o·kā·san mother
おかしい o·ka·shī funny
お金 o·ka·ne money
贈物 o·ku·ri·mo·no gift
遅れ o·ku·re delay ⓝ
起こします o·ko·shi·mas wake (someone) up
おじいさん o·jī·san grandfather

遅い o·soy late
お茶 o·cha tea (Japanese)
夫 ot·to husband
お父さん o·tō·san father
男の子 o·to·ko no ko boy
弟 o·tō·to younger brother
お腹がすいた o·na·ka ga su·i·ta (to be) hungry
お兄さん o·nī·san older brother
お姉さん o·nē·san older sister
おばあさん o·bā·san grandmother
おばさん o·ba·san aunt
お風呂 o·fu·ro bath ⓝ
お土産 o·mi·ya·ge souvenir
オムツ o·mu·tsu diaper • nappy
重い o·moy heavy
降ります o·ri·mas get off (a train, etc)
オレンジ o·ren·ji orange (colour) • orange (fruit)
おわり o·wa·ri end ⓝ
温泉 on·sen mineral hot-spring spa
女の子 on·na no ko girl

か ka

ガールフレンド gā·ru·fu·ren·do girlfriend
階 kai floor (storey)
海外 kai·gai abroad • overseas
外国の gai·ko·ku no foreign
会社 kai·sha company (firm)
快速 kai·so·ku rapid train
階段 kai·dan stairway
ガイド gai·do guide (person)
ガイド付きツアー gai·do·tsu·ki·tsu·ā guided tour
ガイドブック gai·do·buk·ku guidebook
買います kai·mas buy
買い物をします kai·mo·no o shi·mas shop ⓥ
顔 ka·o face
鏡 ka·ga·mi mirror
鍵 ka·gi key
書きます ka·ki·mas write

81

JAPANESE to ENGLISH

鍵をかけた ka·gi o ka·ke·ta locked
鍵をかけます ka·gi o ka·ke·mas lock ⓥ
カクテル ka·ku·te·ru cocktail
かさ ka·sa umbrella
貸します ka·shi·mas rent ⓥ
家族 ka·zo·ku family
ガソリン ga·so·rin gas • petrol
ガソリンスタンド ga·so·rin·stan·do petrol station • service station
肩 ka·ta shoulder
片道切 ka·ta·mi·chi·kip·pu one-way ticket
月 ga·tsu month
カップ kap·pu cup
彼女の ka·no·jo no her (ownership)
彼女は ka·no·jo wa she
彼女を ka·no·jo o her (as object of sentence)
かばん ka·ban bag
カフェ ka·fe cafe
カプセルホテル ka·pu·se·ru·ho·te·ru capsule hotel
花粉症 ka·fun·shō hay fever
紙 ka·mi paper
剃刀 ka·mi·so·ri razor
剃刀の刃 ka·mi·so·ri no ha razor blade
カメラ ka·me·ra camera
かゆみ ka·yu·mi itch ⓝ
から ka·ra from
空の ka·ra no empty
軽い ka·ru·i light (not heavy) ⓐ
彼は ka·re wa he
皮 ka·wa leather ⓝ
川 ka·wa river
乾いた ka·wai·ta dry ⓐ
乾かします ka·wa·ka·shi·mas dry (clothes) ⓥ
為替 ka·wa·se currency exchange
観光案内所 kan·kō·an·nai·jo tourist office
感謝している kan·sha shi·te i·ru grateful
勘定 kan·jō bill (restaurant etc) ⓝ
感触 kan·sho·ku feeling (physical)
幹線道路 kan·sen·dō·ro highway
黄色い kī·roy yellow
気温 ki·on temperature (weather)

聴きます ki·ki·mas listen (to)
季節 ki·se·tsu season
北 ki·ta north
喫煙 ki·tsu·en smoking ⓐ
切符 kip·pu ticket
切符売り場 kip·pu·u·ri·ba ticket office
切符販売 kip·pu·ham·bai·ki ticket machine
のう ki·nō yesterday
キャンセル kyan·se·ru cancel ⓥ
休暇 kyū·ka holidays • vacation
救急 kyū·kyū emergency
救急車 kyū·kyū·sha ambulance
救急箱 kyū·kyū·ba·ko first-aid kit
宮殿 kyū·den palace
救命胴衣 kyū·mē·dōy life jacket
今日 kyō today
禁煙 kin·en no nonsmoking
境界 kyō·kai border
教会 kyō·kai church
教師 kyō·shi teacher
兄弟 kyō·dai brother
キロ（グラム) ki·ro(·gu·ra·mu) kilo(gram)
キロメートル ki·ro·mē·to·ru kilometre
金 kin gold ⓝ
銀 gin silver ⓝ
禁煙の kin·en no nonsmoking
緊急の kin·kyū no urgent
航空 kō·kū airline
空港 kū·kō airport
空港税 kū·kō·zē airport tax
航空便 kū·kū·bin airmail
薬 ku·su·ri drug (medicine) • medication
果物 ku·da·mo·no fruit
靴 ku·tsu shoe
靴下 ku·tsu·shi·ta socks
首 ku·bi neck
クレジットカード ku·re·jit·to·kā·do credit card
グラス gu·ra·su glass (for drinking)
グラム gu·ra·mu gram
クリーニング ku·rī·nin·gu cleaning ⓝ
クリーム ku·rī·mu cream
車椅子 ku·ru·ma·i·su wheelchair
クリスマス ku·ri·su·mas Christmas

82

黒い ku·roy black
警察 kē·sa·tsu police
警察署 kē·sa·tsu·sho police station
軽食 ke·sho·ku snack
携帯電話 kē·tai·den·wa mobile phone
ゲイの gē no gay ⓐ
けが ke·ga injury ⓝ
下痢 ge·ri diarrhoea
現金 gen·kin cash ⓝ
言語 gen·go language
建築 ken·chi·ku architecture
公園 kō·en park ⓝ
工学 kō·ga·ku engineering
交換 kō·kan exchange ⓝ
交換します kō·kan shi·mas
exchange ⓥ
航空便 kō·kū·bin flight
工芸品 kō·gē·hin crafts
公衆トイレ kō·shū·toy·re public toilet
香水 kō·su·i perfume
抗生剤 kō·sē·zai antibiotics
紅茶 kō·cha tea (Western)
コート kō·to coat • court (tennis)
コーヒー kō·hī coffee
氷 kō·ri ice
午後 go·go afternoon
ここで ko·ko de here
ごみ箱 go·mi·ba·ko garbage can
これ ko·re this (one)
壊れやすい ko·wa·re·ya·su·i fragile
コンタクトレンズ kon·ta·ku·to·ren·zu
contact lenses
コンドーム kon·dō·mu condom
コンビニ kom·bi·ni convenience store
故障した ko·shō·shi·ta broken down
故障中 ko·shō·chū out of order
子供 ko·do·mo child • children
ごはん go·han rice (cooked)
小道 ko·mi·chi path
ゴルフ go·ru·fu golf
これ ko·re this (one)
壊れた ko·wa·re·ta broken
壊れやすい ko·wa·re·ya·su·i fragile
コンサート kon·sā·to concert
コンドーム kon·dō·mu condom
コンビニ kom·bi·ni convenience store
今夜 kon·ya tonight

さ sa

サービス sā·bis service
サービス料 sā·bis·ryō service charge
最高の sai·kō no best
最後の sai·go no last (final)
祭日 sai·ji·tsu public holiday
(厳格な)菜食主義者 (gen·ka·ku na)
sai·sho·ku·shu·gi·sha vegan
サイズ sai·zu size (general)
財布 sai·fu purse • wallet
魚 sa·ka·na fish
酒屋 sa·ka·ya liquor store
酒 sa·ke alcoholic drink • sake
茶道 sa·dō tea ceremony
寒い sa·mu·i cold (atmosphere)
さん ·san Mr • Mrs • Ms • Miss
幸せな shi·a·wa·se na happy
シーツ shī·tsu bed linen • sheet (bed)
時間 ji·kan hour
時間どおり ji·kan·dō·ri on time
事故 ji·ko accident
時刻表 ji·ko·ku·hyō timetable
辞書 ji·sho dictionary
下着 shi·ta·gi underwear
試着室 shi·cha·ku·shi·tsu changing
room (in shop)
支払い shi·ha·rai payment
島 shi·ma island
ジム ji·mu gym (place)
地元 ji·mo·to local ⓐ
写真 sha·shin photo • photography
シャツ sha·tsu shirt
住所 jū·sho address
週末 shū·ma·tsu weekend
出発 shup·pa·tsu departure
正午 shō·go midday • noon
消臭剤 shō·shū·zai deodorant
消毒剤 shō·do·ku·zai antiseptic ⓝ
情報 jō·hō information
食事 sho·ku·ji meal
女性 jo·sē female • woman
処方箋 sho·hō·sen prescription
城 shi·ro castle
白い shi·roy white
新幹線 shin·kan·sen bullet train

水筒 su·i·tō water bottle
スーツケース sūts·kēs suitcase
スーパー sū·pā supermarket
スカート skā·to skirt
好きです su·ki des like ⓥ
すぐに su·gu ni soon
涼しい su·zu·shī cool (temperature)
勧めます su·su·me·mas recommend ⓥ
頭痛 zu·tsū headache
素晴らしい su·ba·ra·shī great (fantastic)
ズボン zu·bon pants • trousers
生徒 sē·to student
生理用ナプキン sē·ri·yō·na·pu·kin panty liners • sanitary napkins
セーター sē·tā jumper • sweater
席 se·ki seat (place)
セックス sek·kus sex
石鹸 sek·ken soap
接続 se·tsu·zo·ku connection (transport)
背中 se·na·ka back (body part)
セルフサービスの se·ru·fu·sā·bis no self service
洗濯場 sen·ta·ku·ba laundry (place)
銭湯 sen·tō bath house • public baths
そこに so·ko ni there
外側の so·to·ga·wa no outside

た ta

大学 dai·ga·ku university
退屈な tai·ku·tsu na boring
大使館 tai·shi·kan embassy
台所 dai·do·ko·ro kitchen
大切な tai·se·tsu na important
太陽 tai·yō sun
高い ta·kai expensive • high
タクシー tak·shī taxi
たすけ tas·ke help
タバコ ta·ba·ko cigarette
食べます ta·be·mas eat
食べ物 ta·be·mo·no food
だれ da·re who

誕生日 tan·jō·bi birthday • date of birth
ダンス dan·su dancing ⓝ
タンポン tam·pon tampon
血 chi blood
小さい chī·sai small
チーズ chī·zu cheese
チェックイン chek·ku·in check-in (desk)
違う chi·ga·u different
近く chi·ka·ku close • near • nearby
地下鉄 chi·ka·te·tsu subway/metro
地下鉄の駅 chi·ka·te·tsu no eki subway/metro station
地図 chi·zu map
中央 chū·ō centre
昼食 chū·sho·ku lunch
超過 chō·ka excess (baggage)
朝食 chō·sho·ku breakfast
直接に cho·ku·se·tsu ni direct
チョコレート cho·ko·rē·to chocolate
賃貸します chin·tai shi·mas hire
鎮痛剤 chin·tsū·zai painkiller
ツアー tsu·ā tour
疲れた tsu·ka·re·ta tired
つぎ tsu·gi next
妻 tsu·ma wife
冷たい tsu·me·tai cold (to the touch) ⓐ
釣り tsu·ri fishing ⓝ
手 te hand
で de at
出かけます de·ka·ke·mas go out
出口 de·gu·chi exit ⓝ
デザート de·zā·to dessert
手荷物 te·ni·mo·tsu baggage • luggage
手荷物許容量 te·ni·mo·tsu·kyo·yo·ryo baggage allowance
デパート de·pā·to department store
手袋 te·bu·ku·ro gloves
寺 te·ra temple
電車 den·sha train
電池 den·chi battery (general)
電話 den·wa telephone • phone call ⓝ
トイレ toy·re toilet
搭乗券 tō·jō·ken boarding pass
独身の do·ku·shin single (person)
どこ do·ko where
どちら do·chi·ra which

友達 to·mo·da·chi friend
鶏肉 to·ri·ni·ku chicken (meat)
ドレス do·res dress

な *na*

ナイトクラブ nai·to·ku·ra·bu nightclub
ナイフ nai·fu knife
ナイフとフォーク nai·fu to fō·ku
cutlery (lit: knife and fork)
なか na·ka in
長い na·gai long
眺め na·ga·me view
なくした na·ku·shi·ta lost (item)
なしで na·shi de without
なぜ na·ze why
夏 na·tsu summer
なに na·ni what
何もない na·ni·mo nai nothing
ナプキン na·pu·kin napkin
名前 na·ma·e name ⓝ
南京錠 nan·kin·jō padlock
2 ni two
におい ni·oy smell ⓝ
肉 ni·ku meat
肉屋 ni·ku·ya butcher's shop
西 ni·shi west
2週間 ni·shū·kan fortnight
日記 nik·ki diary
日中 nit·chū day
ニュージーランド nyū·jī·ran·do New
Zealand
入場料 nyū·jō·ryō admission (price)
ニュース nyū·su news
庭 ni·wa garden
妊娠している nin·shin shi·te i·ru
pregnant
盗まれた nu·su·ma·re·ta stolen
値段 ne·dan price •
熱 ne·tsu heat • fever
寝袋 ne·bu·ku·ro sleeping bag
眠ります ne·mu·ri·mas sleep ⓥ
練り歯磨き ne·ri·ha·mi·ga·ki toothpaste
年 nen year
年金者 nen·kin·sha pensioner

捻挫 nen·za sprain ⓝ
脳しんとう nō·shin·tō concussion
ノート nō·to notebook (paper)
乗って not·te aboard
のど no·do throat
のどが渇い no·do ga ka·wai·ta (to be)
thirsty
飲みます no·mi·mas drink ⓥ
飲み物 no·mi·mo·no drink ⓝ
乗り換え no·ri·ka·e transfer ⓝ
乗ります no·ri·mas board (a plane,
ship etc)
乗り物酔い no·ri·mo·no·yoy travel
sickness

は *ha*

バー bā bar
はい hai yes
廃墟 hai·kyo ruins
ハイキング hai·kin·gu hiking ⓝ
歯痛 ha·shi·tsu toothache
入ります hai·ri·mas enter
吐き気 ha·ki·ke nausea
博物館 ha·ku·bu·tsu·kan museum
橋 ha·shi bridge
箸 ha·shi (pair of) chopsticks
(市)バス (shi·)bas bus (city)
バスターミナル bas·tā·mi·na·ru bus
station
バス停 bas·tē bus stop
パスポート pas·pō·to passport
パスポート番号 pas·pō·to·ban·gō
passport number
バックパック bak·ku·pak·ku backpack
バッゲージクレーム bag·gē·ji·ku·rē·mu
baggage claim
鼻 ha·na nose
花屋 ha·na·ya florist
パブ pa·bu·pub (bar)
歯ブラシ ha·bu·ra·shi toothbrush
速い ha·yai fast
早く ha·ya·ku early
春 ha·ru spring (season)
晩 ban evening

パン pan bread
晩ごはん ban·go·han dinner
パン屋 pan·ya bakery
ヒーター hī·tā heater
ビーチ bī·chi beach
ビール bī·ru beer
日陰 hi·ka·ge shade
東 hi·ga·shi east
低い hi·ku·i short (height)
ひざ hi·za knee
ビザ bi·za visa
ビジネス bi·ji·nes business
美術館 bi·ju·tsu·kan art gallery
左 hi·da·ri left (direction)
日付 hi·zu·ke date (day)
人 hi·to person • human being
病院 byō·in hospital
病気の byō·ki no ill • sick
美容師 bi·yō·shi hairdresser
昼ごはん hi·ru·go·han lunch
ビン bin bottle
ピンクの pin·ku no pink
不安な fu·an na uncomfortable
プール pū·ru swimming pool
不可能な fu·ka·nō na impossible
腹痛 fu·ku·tsū stomachache
含んで fu·kun·de included
太った fu·tot·ta fat ⓐ
ふとん fu·ton futon
船 fu·ne boat
冬 fu·yu winter
ブラジャー bu·ra·jā bra
フリーマーケット fu·rī·mā·ket·to
fleamarket
プリンタ pu·rin·ta printer (computer)
古い fu·ru·i old
ブレーキ bu·rē·ki brakes
フレーズブック fu·rē·zu·buk·ku
phrasebook
プレゼント pu·re·zen·to present
(gift) ⓝ
プラットフォーム pu·rat·to·fō·mu
platform
風呂場 fu·ro·ba bathroom
分 fun minute
ペニシリン pe·ni·shi·rin penicillin
ペニス pe·nis penis

部屋 he·ya room
方向 hō·kō direction
宝石 hō·se·ki jewellery
帽子 bō·shi hat
保険 ho·ken insurance
墓地 bo·chi cemetery
ホテル ho·te·ru hotel
ホモ ho·mo homosexual ⓝ
本 hon book ⓝ
本屋 hon·ya bookshop
翻訳します hon·ya·ku shi·mas
translate

ま ma

毎 mai every
毎 mai per (day etc)
毎日 mai·ni·chi daily
前 ma·e before
前の ma·e no last (previous)
枕 ma·ku·ra pillow
孫 ma·go grandchild
また ma·ta again
待合室 ma·chi·ai·shi·tsu transit lounge
• waiting room
待ちます ma·chi·mas wait (for) ⓥ
マッチ mat·chi matches (for lighting)
窓 ma·do window
漫画 man·ga comics
右 mi·gi right (direction) ⓐ
短い mi·ji·kai short (length)
水 mi·zu water
湖 mi·zū·mi lake
水着 mi·zu·gi swimsuit
店 mi·se shop ⓝ
道 mi·chi street • road
緑の mi·do·ri no green
南 mi·na·mi south
身分証明 mi·bun·shō·mē
identification
耳 mi·mi ear
みんな min·na everyone
息子 mu·su·ko son
娘 mu·su·me daughter
眼鏡 me·ga·ne glasses (spectacles)

珍しい me·zu·ra·shī rare (uncommon)
メニュー me·nyū menu
毛布 mō·fu blanket
目的地 mo·ku·te·ki·chi destination
もっと mot·to more
もどります mo·do·ri·mas return (come back) ⓥ
森 mo·ri forest

や ya

野菜 ya·sai vegetable
安い ya·su·i cheap
山 ya·ma mountain
夕食 yū·sho·ku dinner
雪 yu·ki snow
ゆっくり yuk·ku·ri slowly
指 yu·bi finger
指輪 yu·bi·wa ring (on finger) ⓝ
夜明け yo·a·ke dawn
夜遊び yo·a·so·bi night out
ヨーロッパ yō·rop·pa Europe
横 yo·ko beside
酔った yot·ta drunk ⓐ
予約 yo·ya·ku appointment • reservation (booking)
より大きい yo·ri ō·kī bigger
より小さい yo·ri chī·sai smaller
より良い yo·ri yoy better
夜 yo·ru night

ら ra

来(月) rai(·ge·tsu) next (month)
ライター rai·tā cigarette lighter
ラジオ ra·ji·o radio

ラップトップ rap·pu·top·pu laptop
離婚した ri·kon shi·ta divorced
離乳食 ri·nyū·sho·ku baby food
リネン ri·nen linen (sheets etc)
リフト ri·fu·to chairlift (skiing)
リモコン ri·mo·kon remote control
リフト ri·fu·to chairlift (skiing)
領事館 ryō·ji·kan consulate
両親 ryō·shin parents
両方 ryō·hō both
旅館 ryo·kan traditional Japanese inn
冷蔵庫 rē·zō·ko fridge • refrigerator
レシート re·shī·to receipt
レズ re·zu lesbian ⓝ
レストラン res·to·ran restaurant
レンズ ren·zu lens
レンタカー ren·ta·kā car hire
ローカル線 rō·ka·ru·sen local train (country)
ロッカー rok·kā luggage lockers
ロッカー rok·kā luggage lockers
露天風呂 ro·tem·bu·ro open-air baths

わ wa

ワイン wain wine
分け合います wa·ke·ai·mas share (with)
私たちの wa·ta·shi·ta·chi no our
私の wa·ta·shi no my
私は wa·ta·shi wa I
私を wa·ta·shi o me
割引 wa·ri·bi·ki discount
悪い wa·ru·i bad

Acknowledgments
Associate Product Director Angela Tinson
Product Editor Shona Gray
Language Writers Yoshi Abe, Keiko Hagiwara
Cover Designer Campbell McKenzie

Thanks
Kate Chapman, Gwen Cotter, Laura Crawford, James Hardy,
Indra Kilfoyle, Kate Mathews, Wibowo Rusli, Juan Winata

Published by Lonely Planet Global Ltd
CRN 554153

1st Edition – June 2018
Text © Lonely Planet 2018
Cover Image Shibuya Crossing, Tokyo, Jan Christopher Becke/AWL ©

Printed in China   10 9 8 7 6 5 4 3 2 1

Contact lonelyplanet.com/contact

Although the authors and Lonely Planet try to make the information as accurate as possible, we accept no responsibility for any loss, injury or inconvenience sustained by anyone using this book.

Paper in this book is certified against the Forest Stewardship Council™ standards. FSC™ promotes environmentally responsible, socially beneficial and economically viable management of the world's forests.

Index

INDEX

Hiragana & Katakana Script Table

あ a ア	い i イ	う u ウ	え e エ	お o オ
か ka カ	き ki キ	く ku ク	け ke ケ	こ ko コ
さ sa サ	し shi シ	す su ス	せ se セ	そ so ソ
た ta タ	ち chi チ	つ tsu ツ	て te テ	と to ト
な na ナ	に ni ニ	ぬ nu ヌ	ね ne ネ	の no ノ
は ha ハ	ひ hi ヒ	ふ fu フ	へ he ヘ	ほ ho ホ
ま ma マ	み mi ミ	む mu ム	め me メ	も mo モ
や ya ヤ		ゆ yu ユ		よ yo ヨ
ら ra ラ	り ri リ	る ru ル	れ re レ	ろ ro ロ
わ wa ワ				を o ヲ
ん n ン				

きゃ kya キャ	きゅ kyu キュ	きょ kyo キョ
しゃ sha シャ	しゅ shu シュ	しょ sho ショ
ちゃ cha チャ	ちゅ chu チュ	ちょ cho チョ
にゃ nya ニャ	にゅ nyu ニュ	にょ nyo ニョ
ひゃ hya ヒャ	ひゅ hyu ヒュ	ひょ hyo ヒョ
みゃ mya ミャ	みゅ myu ミュ	みょ myo ミョ
りゃ rya リャ	りゅ ryu リュ	りょ ryo リョ
ぎゃ gya ギャ	ぎゅ gyu ギュ	ぎょ gyo ギョ
じゃ ja ジャ	じゅ ju ジュ	じょ jo ジョ

が ga ガ	ぎ gi ギ	ぐ gu グ	げ ge ゲ	ご go ゴ
ざ za ザ	じ ji ジ	ず zu ズ	ぜ ze ゼ	ぞ zo ゾ
だ da ダ	ぢ ji ヂ	づ zu ヅ	で de デ	ど do ド
ば ba バ	び bi ビ	ぶ bu ブ	べ be ベ	ぼ bo ボ
ぱ pa パ	ぴ pi ピ	ぷ pu プ	ぺ pe ペ	ぽ po ポ

びゃ bya ビャ	びゅ byu ビュ	びょ byo ビョ
ぴゃ pya ピャ	ぴゅ pyu ピュ	ぴょ pyo ピョ

10 Phrases to Get You Talking

Hello.	こんにちは。 kon·ni·chi·wa
Goodbye.	さようなら。 sa·yō·na·ra
Please.	ください。 ku·da·sai
Thank you.	ありがとう。 a·ri·ga·tō
Excuse me.	すみません。 su·mi·ma·sen
Sorry.	ごめんなさい。 go·men·na·sai
Yes.	はい。 hai
No.	いいえ。 ī·ye
I don't understand.	わかりません。 wa·ka·ri·ma·sen
How much is it?	おいくらですか? o·i·ku·ra des ka